Advance Praise for *Never Too Late*

"Only Roy Rowan could have written this book: part world tour, part excursion into the human body. From war zones to political conventions, from baseball to anti-inflammatories, from Mao to Mark Twain, this is the stuff of life, and a how-to guide to growing older . . . in great fashion!"
—Brian Williams, NBC News

"Roy Rowan is not exactly like you and me: he fought in one war and covered three others, palled around with presidents, ran the New York marathon, and survived three cancers. But out of all these adventures and crises, he has written a book that is marvelously beneficial to every one of us on the far side of middle age. Do not go gentle, he insists, but live with the three E's, Enthusiasm, Exertion, and Energy. If you do, Scouts Honor, you'll move up the alphabet to wonder years of Pride, Productivity, and Passion."
—Richard B. Stolley, founding editor of *People* magazine, and senior editorial adviser at Time Inc.

"You can't be too old—or too young—not to enjoy *Never Too Late*. Roy Rowan's advice to us pre-boomers isn't just uplifting. Even better: it's downright practical."
—Frank Deford, author of *Bliss, Remembered*

"This adventure and wisdom-packed book is a boon to seniors who will no longer need to apologize for the space they take up on the planet. It will also help the young prepare for geezerhood."
—Albert Rosenfeld, author of *Prolongevity II*

"There's enough adventure in this book to keep your heart pounding deep into your senior years. As an accomplished field reporter and journalist, Roy Rowan has seen the front lines of combat, talked with dictators, and lived (temporarily) as a vagabond to report on our homeless problem. And this book captures all of his energy, spirit, curiosity, and wisdom. It's packed with vivid stories, wonderful quotes, and wise comments to show how growing old can be just as exciting and fulfilling as any other part of living. I hope I'm like Roy Rowan when I'm 90. He rocks. And we can too. It's a wonderful read."

—Helen Fisher, anthropologist at Rutgers University, and author of *Why Him? Why Her?*

"Want to learn how to age gracefully and have a great retirement? Then this is NOT the book for you! Roy Rowan, a great journalist, offers instead delightful tales and lessons about having a feisty and active old age. It's both a charming memoir and a fountain of insight for anyone who plans to live until at least 100."

—Walter Isaacson, president of the Aspen Institute, and author of biographies of Albert Einstein and Ben Franklin

Never Too Late

A 90-Year-Old's Pursuit of a Whirlwind Life

ROY ROWAN

LYONS PRESS
Guilford, Connecticut
An imprint of Globe Pequot Press

Lyons Press is an imprint of Globe Pequot Press.
Illustration on page viii © Gerald Dumas
Text design by Sheryl P. Kober

Library of Congress Cataloging-in-Publication Data

Rowan, Roy.
  Never too late : a 90-year-old's pursuit of a whirlwind life / Roy Rowan.
    p. cm.
  ISBN 978-0-7627-6376-4
  1. Older people. 2. Aging. I. Title.
  HQ1061.R65 2010
  305.260973—dc22

                                                                2010050814

Printed in the United States of America

10 9 8 7 6 5 4 3 2 1

For Helen and her indomitable spirit

Contents

"So, I hear you're retired."

"Few people know how to be old."
—François, Duc de La Rochefoucauld
(1613–1680)

*"We turn not older with years,
but new every day."*
—Emily Dickinson
(1830–1886)

Who Says You Have to Grow Old Gracefully!

Libraries are filled with volumes containing recipes for growing old gracefully. Most of them are based on mountains of research and statistics provided by doctors, gerontologists, and physical therapists. I have read many of these books, and without question, they are full of helpful suggestions for living long and productively.

This book, however, is no such manual. It is simply one ninety-year-old man's views of the pleasures and potentials of old age based on a long life crammed full of adventures as a correspondent for *Time*, *Life*, and *Fortune* magazines. And, I should add, the lessons learned along the way from diverse groups of people, from the world's most powerful leaders to the world's most pitiful individuals—the homeless men and women living on the streets of New York.

Readers be warned! This feisty man's guide to growing old, written in the form of a rambling memoir, is about aging, vigorously, actively, and any way but gracefully. I subscribe to the view expressed by the Welsh poet, Dylan Thomas:

Do not go gentle into that good night,
Old age should burn and rave at close of day;
Rage, rage against the dying of the light.
Do not go gentle into that good night.

{1}

How Old Is Old?

She was so pretty, her face etched in sadness, peering out the window of the bus. I guess my admiring stare caught her by surprise, because suddenly her face brightened as she stood up and offered me her seat.

"Really! Do I look that old and tottery?" I thought. No woman had ever done that before. And why should they? My barber tells me my hair is thicker than most guys half my age. My doctor says I have a much younger man's body. Even my kids believe I'm still sharp enough to conquer all the complicated electronic equipment they give me for Christmas. And it wasn't eons ago that these same two legs I am now standing on carried me through all twenty-six miles, three hundred and eighty-five yards of the New York City Marathon. Sure, Bill Rogers had already crossed the finish line when I hit the halfway mark. But finishing in good form, not winning, was my sole objective. Sort of the way I look at life.

"Please," the young woman said, smiling and pointing to her vacated seat. Not a sexy come-hither smile, but a benign half-smile reserved for men rendered harmless by their advanced years. Again I thought, "Do I really look so impotent and non-threatening? How would she have reacted if I'd said, 'Thanks, but why don't we get off this rattletrap and go have a drink?' Wouldn't that have stunned her!" Not that I drink much. Maybe a glass of pinot noir before dinner now and then.

"Thank you, I'm fine," I said, declining the empty seat as the young woman pushed her way forward through the pack of standees at the front of the bus. That was ten years ago. But it made such an impression that I can still see the nonplussed look on her face when I remained standing and another woman quickly sat down in her place.

Today, at ninety, I've become reconciled to young women getting up and offering me their seats. Pride or plain stubbornness keeps me from accepting, even though a few twinges in those two marathon-proven legs often say, "Shut up and sit down!" But that would be giving up on a body that has refused to surrender to two bouts of cancer, or one that continues to get up before sunrise to cast a fishing line into the surf, or is game to fly around the world to revisit the old haunts covered years ago as a correspondent for *Time*, *Life*, and *Fortune*.

Perhaps there's a more subconscious reason for my refusing to accept these proffered seats—not just to show that I'm still steady on my feet, but to stand up for old age as a vibrant and productive time of life. So many of my contemporaries have let their bodies (and sometimes their brains) disintegrate as if that was to be expected during what they facetiously call their "golden years." A few even take pride in enumerating their ailments in what some wag called "organ recitals."

True, I'm not running around in high gear as I used to, with all my worldly possessions packed in one carry-on suitcase. The hunger for adventure that drew me to Mao's revolution in China more than sixty years ago, and then to both the Korean and Vietnam wars, has been sated. Flying out of Saigon on one of the last helicopters on April 30, 1975 came as a welcome finale to my years of combat reporting, even though I still feel my adrenaline surge while reliving those wars in my writings.

I've also given up chasing after the likes of Generalissimo Chiang Kai-shek or former Communist Premier Zhou Enlai for frontline interviews. Or seeking private dinners with foreign leaders like Philippine president Ferdinand Marcos and his wife Imelda in Manila's glittering Malacanang Palace. Or accompanying the Pope or Billy Graham on their evangelist tours abroad. Those exhilarating experiences, all stored safely in my memory bank, remain fascinating to look back on. Oddly enough, so are a few of the maddening frustrations that went with the job of prying stories from people who shunned publicity, individuals such as Mafia kingpin Tony Salerno or Teamster boss Jimmy Hoffa. Today, those attempted stone-wallings have melted in memory into routine problems that went with the job.

Other things that used to rankle me also now seem unimportant. For one, *Life* photographers on our dangerous joint assignments were paid more than us reporters even though we both ran the same risks. "Photographers are like baseball players," the managing editor explained. "Their legs go at forty." Little did he reckon that Carl Mydans, Gordon Parks, Alfred Eisenstaedt, David Douglas Duncan, Cartier-Bresson, and some of the other *Life* and freelance superstars I was teamed up with (and whose camera bags I carried on various assignments), never got the word and were still shooting pictures well into their nineties.

"Why don't you slow down and enjoy life?" friends keep asking. "Actually, I have," I tell them. I walk instead of jogging, write without accepting crushing deadlines, and delight in spending hours sprawled on the floor with my ten-year-old grandson building towering structures with his Legos. But as for "enjoying life," those well-meaning friends don't understand that for me it means doing the things I've always done. More slowly, for sure, but more thoughtfully too, often mixing reminiscences with the job at hand. My heroes are not the corporate titans that I once wrote about for *Fortune* whose golden parachutes landed them safely inside gated retirement communities for unbroken days of golf, bridge, and sunsets seen through a martini glass. No, my models are the two Pablos—Picasso and Casals—who pursued their painting and cello-playing into their nineties.

"When did you retire?" strangers often ask. That seems to be a popular opening gambit at social gatherings in my hometown of Greenwich, Connecticut. "In 1985," I tell them, because that's when I left my full-time writing job at Time Incorporated. Most of them would consider it crazy that my daily routine hasn't changed much since then: up at five, write, work out with weights, eat breakfast, write some more until it's time for a late lunch, followed by an afternoon walk with my wife Helen.

We combine these meanderings with stops to view all the new construction, mainly condos for recent retirees. Once primarily a bedroom community for commuters, Greenwich is becoming a haven for those who've quit work but refuse to move into one of those beautifully manicured assisted-living meccas with bucolic names like Sterling Glen, Edge Hill,

Pleasant Valley, and Meadow Ridge. There are more than thirty-six thousand assisted living residences in the U.S., caring for just over one million people. "Live the dream, an uncompromising lifestyle awaits you," one of their typical promotions promises. But as far as I'm concerned, they can keep on waiting. (Although I must admit the Anthem Ranch, a retirement community in Broomfield, Colorado, advertises some rather intriguing activities, including snowshoeing, rock climbing, and skydiving—the latter sport, I suspect, being offered to those eager to undergo the ultimate old-persons' stress test of jumping out of an airplane, as President George H. W. Bush did on his eightieth birthday, or blasting back into orbit aboard the space shuttle as former astronaut and retired senator John Glenn did at the age of seventy-seven.)

My favorite sport, surfcasting, is more of a stress-reducing test. During summers on Block Island my early mornings are reserved for fishing off the beach, a contemplative hour or two when catching something isn't as important as watching the stars fade as the sun's fireball rises out of the sea, setting everything ablaze. Most mornings this rhythmical motion of swinging a rod back and forth and watching a brightly painted lure go flying into a wave goes for naught, or only for exercise. But if by chance a fish strikes, the primordial message coming from this wild creature at the other end of the line is more meaningful now that my own days are numbered: "You and I, Mr. Fisherman, though temporarily tied together, are engaged in a deadly duel of endurance that only one of us can win." The fish's vast capacity for courage and will to live is the same power, I believe, that propels people through a long and successful life.

My idea for achieving this, as I mentioned, is to keep on doing the same things that motivated me in my younger years—some that generate a sense of accomplishment, others that simply provide relaxation or pleasure. My worst fear is being overcome by a feeling of obsolescence. So many men and women of the arts, I've read, feel the same way. Even if their work demands exhausting physical effort, they refuse to stop. Once Alexander Calder, the artist famous for his huge metal sculptures and mobiles, was asked, "Now that you're older, how do you handle those heavy pieces of steel?" "With elation," he replied instantly.

For me there's no substitute for work, and the joy it can bring. Better than aspirin or Tylenol, it also suppresses the aches and pains of a vintage body, just as it keeps the creative juices flowing. "Work is the scythe of time," claimed Napoleon Bonaparte. And it is that for me, making my years toward my centennial fly by. "Work as if you were to live one hundred years," recommended the multi-talented Ben Franklin. But then, little did Ben realize that the time would soon come when centenarians would comprise the fastest growing segment of the U.S. population. More than one-hundred thousand (90 percent of them women) are estimated to be alive and well. And their numbers are expected to more than double in the next twenty years.

Old comedians have a sly way of dodging the age factor and recognizing the possibility that they might not be around much longer. George Burns was approaching his hundredth birthday and still performing when someone asked him if he was worried about dying. "Me? I can't die," he snapped. "I'm booked." Woody Allen voiced what many feel: "I don't mind the idea of dying. I just don't want to be there when it happens." There may be no escaping being present at your own death, but I'd like to think that I'll still be booked to write more books at my century mark.

Sometimes while riding a bus, I'm reminded of that pretty young woman who so abruptly made me aware of my age. How did she pick me out of the crowd as needing a seat? It's not as if our bodies bear visible proof of our age like a tree's cambial rings or a male elk's antlers. Nevertheless most of our years are spent in a world populated by people older than we are, so we are not accustomed to being viewed as old. Even the celebrated French novelist Andre Gide admitted, "I have to make a great effort to convince myself that I am at present as old as those who seemed so ancient when I was young."

Still, I take heart in such clichés as "age is only a number" (my wife's, by the way, is unlisted), or that "you're only as old as you feel." Of course, down deep I know that our biological clocks keep ticking. Even so I like to think that ageless philosopher Satchel Paige had it right when he asked, "How old would you be if you didn't know how old you was?"

{2}

Quit Is a Four-Letter Word

Baby boomers used to warn, "Don't trust anybody over thirty." Yet once they got to be thirty their perspective changed. As Isiah Thomas, the former basketball star, remarked as he passed that milestone, "Age isn't what it used to be."

Since most of our lives are spent in a world populated by people older than we are, suddenly finding ourselves in their age bracket takes some getting used to. But we too can change our perspective. Because although the idea of being old someday may have once sounded unpleasant, as Mark Twain said of Richard Wagner's music, "It sounds worse than it is."

Even so, crossing the bridge into your seventies, eighties, or nineties can be especially depressing when the names of famous people younger than you seem to jump off the obituary pages of the newspaper. However, looking at it another way, being a survivor should be cause for celebration—a life that is still yours to be lived.

But don't be misled. As I stated in my author's note, this is not a manual for growing old gracefully, based on facts culled from mountains of research. It's simply one man's views of the pleasures and opportunities of old age based on a long life crammed full of adventures. Some of the lesson came from a long personal association, other times from just a momentary meeting or passing remark that remained etched in my memory forever.

Such a fleeting encounter happened to me on Thanksgiving Day in 1950, the first year of the Korean War. And in a way, as I'll explain, it still goads me on to reach new goals in my advanced years.

A *Life* photographer and I were attached to an American Army unit called Task Force Cooper. The temperature had sunk to twenty-five below zero. Bundled in their clumsy winter clothing, Captain Cooper's exhausted infantrymen were trying to pick their way along the exposed southern face of the Yalu River Gorge separating North Korea from Manchuria in China. A sheer rock wall towered five hundred feet above. Far below, the emerald water of the ice-clogged Yalu slithered like a cold green snake through the bottom of the gorge.

The Chinese were not yet in the war, although their sentries, wearing mustard-colored uniforms, could clearly be seen patrolling up and down in Manchurian territory on the gorge's northern bank. The retreating North Korean troops had burned all the bridges and blasted gaping holes in the cliff-side road that we were on, forcing Captain Cooper to park his tanks and self-propelled 75 mm guns, along with his kitchen truck, three miles back. His immediate objective was a tunnel that would provide protection and a vantage point from which to view the village where the enemy troops were dug in. The tunnel was about a thousand yards ahead. But to reach it the photographer and I would have to run and duck through a barrage of burp gun bullets ricocheting off the cliff. We were crouched behind a boulder waiting for the firing to subside when two medics dove in behind the boulder next to us.

"Look, dearie," said one of the stretcher-bearers to his partner, "we'd better stop here and catch a smoke."

"Okay, honey," agreed the other. From their conversation, I gathered they'd just rescued a soldier who'd been shot in the stomach. Unfortunately, the wounded man had been shot again in the hip as they carried him to safety.

The medic called Honey studied the two cameras dangling from neck straps down the front of the photographer's parka. "Wish I had your job," he finally blurted, his breath billowing clouds of steam as he spoke.

"How come?" I replied. "Here we are on Thanksgiving Day, freezing our asses off together behind the same boulder, hoping we don't get shot."

Honey looked at me like I was crazy. "Yeah," he said. "But if I had your job I'd quit."

We never saw that medic again—he was killed the next day—but his wisecrack about quitting kept echoing through my brain. Of course, he didn't have a clue about what drives us reporters and photographers, the excitement of covering an important military action, and the satisfaction of relaying the news of its outcome to the world. Or how the adrenaline shooting through your veins in pursuit of a dangerous story produces a habit-forming high—a false sense of well-being, almost invulnerability—that propels you into taking greater and greater risks, until if you don't wake up to what's going on you'll end up like the moth consumed by the flame.

I've since seen that happen to two of my *Life* photographer friends. Paul Schutzer was covering the so-called "Six-Day War" in the Sinai Peninsula in 1967. After trying to get ahead of the Israeli soldiers on foot, he decided to take a chance and hitch a ride in one of their tanks leading the assault. The tank was blown up by an Egyptian mortar with Paul in it. During the Vietnam War, Larry Burrows, another *Life* photographer, kept going out on one helicopter gunship raid after another until his luck ran out. In 1971 the last gunship he was on crashed and his remains were only recently found. Quit? Neither one of those two men ever considered doing that and neither did I. *Quit* always had as profane a sound to me as the other nasty four-letter words.

Those days of adrenaline highs covering wars in China, Korea, and Vietnam are long gone for me. The memories of them are even a little blurred, though that medic's quip still occasionally rings in my ears. More than that, it's now become a joke I've used in different ways and on different occasions. It's a great exit line for getting off the podium after giving a speech: I describe the war scene in Korea, and then announce to my audience: "Like the medic said, 'If I had your job I'd quit,' so I'm going to quit talking right now." That always gets a good laugh.

I also used the same punch line to teach my four sons when they were still young the importance of completing a job. And today, faced with many tasks made more challenging by my advanced age—like writing this book—I hear those same words. Somehow they get me back on track, ready to face the job at hand.

After all, one of the biggest problems faced by men and women of my generation is their failure to keep on doing the things that excited them during their younger years. Those who are propelled along by their writing, their art, their music, or whatever it is that inspires them, seem to live the longest. But let's face it, the desire to quit—even in some cases to quit living—can be almost irresistible.

Several of my friends decided their lives were in effect over when they hit seventy or eighty. They quit trying to do the things that gave them joy and satisfaction. "It's too late," is the usual lament. But as Henry Wadsworth Longfellow wrote: "Nothing is too late until the heart shall ccasc to palpitate." Or as Somerset Maugham advised, "It's never too late to be what you might have been."

Look at Jimmy Carter, dubbed the "poster boy of retirement." At the age of seventy-eight, twenty years after losing the White House, he won the Nobel Prize as a global peacemaker. *Falstaff,* Verdi's last opera, was composed when he was eighty. Titian was said to have painted "Christ Crowned with Thorns" at ninety-five. At the incredible age of one hundred and seven, George Abbott collaborated on the revival of the musical *Damn Yankees.*

Women, too, have similarly shown bursts of creativity in their final years. "Granny's left the rocking chair for grad school," is no joke. Mary Fasano, the oldest student ever to graduate from Harvard, was seventy-one when she received her diploma. And Anna Mary Robertson ("Grandma Moses") started painting at seventy-six when arthritis left her unable to hold embroidery needles. She had her first show at eighty.

Remember the Delany sisters? They burst into the limelight in 1992 with the bestseller *Having Our Say:*

The Delany Sisters' First Hundred Years. Sadie was then already one hundred and four and Bessie one hundred and two. Talk about not quitting! These daughters of a slave described their trials and tribulations as blacks trying to build their careers before the civil rights movement. Sadie became the first African American woman allowed to teach home economics in New York State, while sister Bessie became the second black woman awarded a dentistry license there. Their high-spirited story was portrayed on television and spawned a Broadway play. The sisters were also included in the 1993 Guinness Book of Records as the world's oldest authors. But they didn't stop there, and a year later followed with a sequel: *The Delanys' Book of Everyday Wisdom.* After Bessie's death at one hundred and four, Sadie went on to write *On My Own At 107: Reflections on Life Without Bessie.* She died two years later at one hundred and nine. Of course, the Delanys' determination to succeed and to keep churning out books well into their hundreds was unique. They could have called it quits years earlier without making any excuses.

As we all know, quitting many things becomes mandatory long before we hit the century mark. At about eighty I had to stop jogging—"running away from death," as I used to call it—substituting brisk walks instead. My knees were fine, but I didn't have the wind. The arthritis in my shoulders also put an end to push-ups, but not to doing sit-ups, stretches, and shadowboxing every morning with five-pound weights. Working out is tedious, it's time-consuming, it's boring, but it's great. For me, the desire to stay in shape is as strong as ever. It determines how I feel, and hopefully look. But more than that, daily exercise has become as addictive as was the pursuit of an exciting story. On days when it isn't possible to do so, I just don't feel right. Or so I think.

Physical trainers say that you shouldn't look upon a workout as work. "Think of it as a pleasant interlude in your day," one of them told me. I've never quite gotten to considering exercise joyful. It still takes an effort, and sometimes requires the utmost self-discipline not to flop back into bed and skip a morning. It's easy to say to yourself, "Hey, it's Sunday, the day of rest." But that just makes it harder to resume on Monday. Quitting altogether, I fear, is the next step after skipping a day or two.

I've always thought there were more than physical benefits to exercise, that it did more than build muscles and stave off heart disease. And sure enough, it's been established for some time that the endorphin secreted by the brain during exercise combats pain and produces a feeling of well-being. Biochemists have recently discovered that the mental benefits of exercise can also boost brainpower and may even aid in the battle against Alzheimer's.

The process starts in the muscles. Every time a bicep or quad contracts and releases it emits a protein called IGF-1. I've always been skeptical of highly technical explanations of everyday body functions, but the biochemists claim the IGF-1 travels through the bloodstream and triggers the production of several more chemicals, including a molecule called BDNF, which one researcher equates with Miracle-Gro for the brain. And certainly almost everyone over eighty could use a little of that.

Nevertheless, many older people believe they waited too long to reap the benefits of exercise. As Eubie Blake, the great ragtime pianist and composer who lived to be ninety-six, said, "If I'd known I was going to live so long I would have taken better care of myself." But no point in lamenting the fact that you failed to start exercising earlier. The physical trainers will tell you it's never too late.

An overweight friend who shuns exercise as if it were some silly fetish gets testy at my extolling the feeling of well-being, or endorphin high, following a workout. "You enjoy exercising," he snaps, just the way other friends occasionally say to me, "You must really enjoy writing." The truth is, I like to *have* written just as I like to *have* worked out. But the doing of both can be painful. As former sports columnist Red Smith once admitted, "Writing involves staring at a typewriter until drops of blood pop out on your forehead." During a workout it may only be sweat that pops out, but physical therapists say exercise is the best anti-depressant, and without the side effects of drugs.

For many journalists, as well as for other professionals, retirement ("the worst word in the English language," according to Ernest Hemingway) meant quitting the one thing that gave meaning to their lives. One of my closest friends, a reporter for the *Wall Street Journal* for some forty years, could barely wait for the day he could walk away with his retirement package. His wife was even more thrilled with the prospect of his being free for them to do things together. The trouble is they'd done all the necessary financial planning, but neglected to figure out how they were going to spend their time.

It didn't take but a few weeks before he went skipping back to the *Journal* seeking special assignments. For the next year he contributed to a weekly feature describing inventions of the past hundred years (sliced bread was one of them) to celebrate the newspaper's centennial. Then for another year he collaborated on putting the information into a book. His wife got right back in the groove of chatting with her girlfriends on the phone, something she felt constrained about doing when he was sitting at home with her.

The time may come when Americans spend more of their lives retired than working. "We could have a whole generation of people who are healthy, wealthy, and bored," warns Dorothy Cantor, co-author of *What Do You Want to Do When You Grow Up?* For that reason many major corporations are starting to provide free counseling on retirement living for older employees.

One of the most difficult adjustments is no longer having a job title. It's been said that "you are what your job is." Alex Comfort, British gerontologist and author of *The Joy of Sex*, tells of going on a tour of the Capitol building given by a young senator for a group of retired persons. "And what did you used to be?" the senator asked one man. "I still am," the man replied huffily.

This may sound silly, but one retired friend of mine described feeling "naked" when being introduced at parties without his old job title. However, only if you enjoyed a particularly distinguished career can you expect your hostess to remind other guests of what you did for a living. "Meet Bill Davis. He used to be consul-general in Novosibirsk." Or "You remember Janet Smith; she played Gypsy in the original cast." But for rank-and-file retirees, forget it. What you did is history. Nobody at the party cares if Bill Davis ran a dry cleaning chain, or if Janet Smith worked as a dental technician.

Living happily without your old job title, the gerontologists (*geron* is the Greek word for old man) claim, can be made easier by re-tiring the wheels of your career, so to speak, and driving off in a new direction. A one-time hobby can be converted into a full-time pursuit. A friend, formerly a high-powered ad executive, once retired, carved and painted lifelike wooden models of shore birds and sold them for thousands of dollars. A museum is now being constructed on Cape Cod to show his work.

A woman friend who spent all of her vacations traveling abroad went into business leading tour groups to her old European haunts. The archivist at Time Inc. became a voice teacher. An investment banker neighbor has become a high school history teacher, and the former public relations vice president of a *Fortune* 500 company, whom I thought was wedded forever to big business, became a successful artist, showing (and selling) his collages and abstract paintings in galleries in the U.S., France, and Japan. Every one of these friends regrets not having embarked on their second career much sooner.

Launching a second career takes what I call the Three Es: Enthusiasm to try something new, Exertion to actually get started, and the Energy not to quit. Starting is easy. So is quitting after a few false starts. The secret is to keep going until an absorbing interest won't let you turn back.

Breaking out of the old work mold isn't easy. Neither is escaping the web of relationships established over a lifetime in business. (Some former professional relationships are worth keeping. See chapter 7.) It's a lot more comfortable just to relax and follow the path of least resistance. As the late John W. Gardner, an acute observer of American society, wrote in his book, *Self Renewal: The Individual and the Innovative Society*, "Innovation starts with a problem to be solved, and there are lots of problems in old age." The biggest one, he points out, may be how to spend your time.

Fortunately, almost everyone has undeveloped potentialities that can bloom with a little nurturing. In my own case, I started writing books once I retired as a magazine correspondent, writer, and editor. That was an easy step up, not nearly as challenging as jumping into an entirely different field. But when this book, my ninth, is finished, I plan to return to drawing and painting, the hobby of my youth.

When I was an undergraduate at Dartmouth College, artist-in-residence Paul Sample urged me to give up my dream of becoming a foreign correspondent and pursue a career in painting. He claimed to have spotted a creative spark in my pen-and-ink sketches and watercolor paintings made during summer vacations spent working on tankers and cargo ships in the Merchant Marine. But World War II interceded, and after spending four years in the army I was determined to pursue a career in journalism. Frankly, I'm now full of apprehensions about trying to resurrect a latent talent for painting and drawing that I stopped developing seventy years ago. But I'm determined to give it a whirl.

Aside from recycling old hobbies, there's the opportunity to acquire an entirely new skill, like learning a foreign language, or playing a musical instrument, or studying astronomy, or taking up carpentry, weaving, or some other handiwork. Volunteer work can also give structure to the day. The list of possibilities goes on ad infinitum. You don't have to do a lot, but it's important to do something and not just vegetate. Edmund Burke, the eighteenth century British philosopher and statesman, said, "Nothing is more tragic than the man who did nothing because he could only do a little."

On the other hand, British statesman Winston Churchill once remarked, "A man can grow too old, and I am too old." Maybe that's true, but I can't imagine ever feeling that way without suffering from some excruciating pain or dementia or some other ailment that made death a welcome event. Usually, there is something left in life to hold your interest and to look forward to. James Holy Eagle, chief of the Lakota tribe who was born a year before the Wounded Knee Massacre in 1890, said he had to keep on living in pain so he could continue to speak out for his people. He did until a few months before his hundredth birthday.

As you grow older the gerontologists believe it helps to keep a high level of curiosity—about people, politics, foreign affairs, nature, science—all of the things my grandmother used to say "make the world go round." In her nineties she belonged to a group of widows who, despite their dimming sight and hearing, met once a week to discuss world affairs. I would like to believe that I've inherited her curiosity and genes, and that in five or six more years my own interests in the world will continue to be that intense. I believe they will be. As a former reporter, I'm even curious to know what it feels like to die, though I'm happy to wait until the last possible moment to find out.

{3}

R Is for Resilience

"Virtue will have naught to do with ease," wrote Michel de Montaigne, the celebrated sixteenth century French essayist. "It seeks a rough and thorny path." And never is this more true than during life's later years. The road to a ripe and rewarding old age is full of bumps, potholes, and detours, as everyone traveling this route knows. One of the secrets of navigating it successfully, say the specialists in aging, is resiliency—the flexibility to cope with the many setbacks encountered and to enjoy the trip, because the final destination holds little appeal. Even so, we can't help thinking about death now and then. As molecular biologist Dr. John J. Medina pointed out in his book *The Clock of Ages*, "Lying in the back of your mind like a sleeping dog, is the raw fact of your own mortality."

Thoughts of their own mortality never seemed to deter any of the world leaders that I covered during my years as a correspondent. To me their most common characteristic was resiliency. This trait not only helped them in their rise to power, it also contributed to their longevity. Most of them—German Chancellor Adenauer, Marshal Tito of Yugoslavia, Chiang Kaishek, Mao Zedong, Ronald Reagan, and Jerry Ford, to name a few—made it into their eighties or nineties.

Certainly it wasn't only raw ambition that empowered and preserved them. I've covered too many other people who aspired to greatness but got nowhere. Neither was a rich inheritance or a good education the sole reason for their success. The leaders I came to know best were mostly self-made men or women. It was their energy and ability to overcome all setbacks that enabled them to soar higher and higher, instead of stalling in mid-flight.

South Korea's former President Kim Dae Jung, who was awarded the Nobel Prize in 2000 for his steadfast pursuit of democracy, is an example. He was still his country's opposition leader when I last saw him in 1980. Under house arrest, and confined to a dimly lit hovel with a dirt floor, he told me how he'd been physically harassed by the government. "One time," he said, "they blindfolded me on a boat with weights tied to my feet, ready to toss me overboard, when a U.S. helicopter suddenly appeared overhead and saved my life." But during our conversation he kept referring to what he called his "sunshine policy" for promoting his country's bright future. This, he assured me, would eventually convince his countrymen to pick him as their leader, which they finally did in 1997.

Of course, few people are ever forced to undergo that severe a test of stamina and staying power. But it's important to remember there are a number of men and women in our society who lack the ability to surmount even more commonplace setbacks—the loss of a job or money, an illness, the death of a spouse. These can cause some older people to lose hope completely and end up homeless, living in shelters or on the street.

As a writer of several pop-psych articles for *Fortune* and a book about intuition, I have long been intrigued with what gives some individuals the strength and persistence to overcome devastating experiences, while others are totally unable to cope. I decided to try in a most unusual way to find the answer.

"This may sound like a ridiculous offer," I wrote the managing editor of *People* magazine in January, 1990. "But I'd like to take a crack at being homeless and keep a diary of what one sees, feels, and suffers, and how one tries to adapt." Quite a few of the 70,000 homeless in New York City at that time were my age or older, and I was curious how at that late stage in life so many of them could have fallen between the cracks of our affluent society and succumbed to such squalor.

Were they simply not able to deal with old age? Would they ever be able to climb back up? You might argue that they represent extreme cases and should not be considered in a book dedicated to making the most of old age. However, they simply magnify many of the problems that most of us face as we grow older.

My thought was to cover the homeless crisis the same way I had covered wars—by getting down into the trenches, so to speak, with these pitiful people who seemed to have just given up. Other journalists I knew were covering the problem from a safe distance, getting most of their information secondhand from social workers at the city's various relief agencies. I wanted to disguise myself as a homeless man and spend two weeks out on the street.

"Are you sure you really want to do this?" the managing editor wrote back while accepting my offer.

I began the assignment as any reporter would, interviewing the officials who ran the shelters, soup kitchens, "drop-in centers," and other facilities established to alleviate this deplorable municipal problem. After gathering enough information, and learning what to do and what not to do, to keep from being found out, I stopped shaving, pulled together a ratty wardrobe, and took the precaution of getting a gamma globulin shot to ward off hepatitis. I hid $50 in a money belt for emergencies only. Then, leaving my wallet, my wedding ring, my social security card, and all other identification at home, I disappeared into the murky purgatory of the homeless in mid-January, two weeks before my seventieth birthday. Only my wife and my editor knew what I was up to.

I'd heard horror stories about knifings and shootings of old homeless men, mostly senseless attacks by marauding youth packs. One old man sleeping in a wooden crate, I read, had been doused with gasoline and set afire. I also was aware of wild free-for-alls started by crackheads in the armories in Manhattan and Brooklyn that had been converted into huge, hangar-size shelters. I was a bit apprehensive.

My first stop was the Staten Island ferry terminal, which one social worker described to me as a menagerie. Hidden behind a long line of passengers waiting for the next ferry were some sixty or seventy homeless men and women in various states—sitting and sleeping, drunk and sober, bearded and shaved, calm and agitated. An argument was raging between a grizzled black man and a white-haired woman with a hip cast covering her left leg. She slashed at him with one of her crutches until two policemen chased him away. Across the terminal a shoeless old man was menacing two Asian passengers, hollering, "You Jap bastards stole my job." The same two cops started to lead him away, but blaring loudspeakers were calling for police assistance elsewhere. "NYPD to the change booth!" echoed a plea to help a tottering geezer who had been knocked down by youths hurdling the turnstiles.

I suddenly felt like I'd made a horrible mistake. Sharing a soldier's danger as a war correspondent was strangely exhilarating—hunkering down with these derelicts seemed only demeaning. For these men and women who were unable to pull themselves back up, old age was simply a horror.

However, my intent was not to chronicle the tales of the drunks, drug addicts, and mentally disturbed who made up about 80 percent of the homeless population in the city. Rather, I wanted to find out how the old men and women without these debilitating afflictions, who came from typical American families, and who once held good jobs, and lived in decent homes, could have sunk so low.

I was hoping to blend in with all the vagrants that had converted this dilapidated pier into a makeshift hotel. Would my disguise really work? Could I make myself feel really destitute, or would the safety of my temporary plight betray me? I fixed my gaze on a passenger tapping his shoes, impatiently waiting to board a ferry on the way home. He glanced everywhere except at me. That was a good sign. I had joined the estimated three million homeless Americans, who it was said had become invisible to their countrymen.

I must admit they had become largely invisible to me too. On my way into the city to attend the opera or some other event I passed ragged sleeping bodies sprawled over the cold marble floor of Grand Central Terminal almost unnoticed. Yet some of them were dressed well enough to pass for elderly commuters. What had happened to these seemingly sane, reasonably kempt old people who languish in rail and subway stations, bus depots, or bank vestibules, or stand like frozen statues on the street?

I soon met a man who claimed he had lived at the ferry terminal for three weeks. "Years ago I worked for E. F. Hutton," he said, pointing off in the direction of Wall Street where the former brokerage firm was then located. "I commuted every day from Westfield, New Jersey," he added before relating the triple tragedy that had wiped him out both emotionally and financially. His wife died. He lost his job, and a sudden drop in the market caught him with a big margin account in his stock portfolio that left him broke. "I was sixty-nine years old and didn't have the strength to start over again."

I decided to spend the night riding back and forth on the ferry. Its throbbing engines lulled me right to sleep, but as the ferry docked in Staten Island a cop rapped his club against the back of my seat, ordering me to debark. So I had to buy another ticket to ride back to join the snorers in the Manhattan terminal.

When the new day dawned I found myself camped between a pair of talkative New Englanders. One proclaimed himself a lace-curtain Irishman from Boston. His downfall apparently came from growing up with too much money and an unquenchable thirst for whiskey, though he was now off booze completely. Having quit Boston College to join the Army in World War II, he married, as he said, "A very artistic lady, who eventually departed for Palm Beach with my and her money." But I couldn't pry loose the secret that had sent him into oblivion.

My other seatmate was an aging but still twinkle-eyed woman, originally from New Bedford, Massachusetts. She had moved to New York City where her husband drove a taxi. "One night," she said, "he was parked in front of Metropolitan Hospital and was shot and killed by holdup men." For several years after his death she worked in a stationery store but kept falling behind in her rent. Reluctantly, she entered a city shelter, where she said, "I was scared of being robbed or raped, and felt like a prisoner. Here I can walk out through the turnstile and leave any time I want."

In the next two weeks sleeping in shelters (many provided by local churches), eating in soup kitchens, and spending many nights just wandering the streets with the temperature down in the mid-twenties, I encountered a retired Fordham University professor, a onetime female opera singer, a TV actor who played in a show called *The Defenders*, a lawyer, a woman high school teacher with a master's degree, and a handsome middle-aged Trinidadian male fashion model whose photographs had appeared on the covers of several European magazines. He claimed to be the first black man to have modeled clothes on the runways of Europe for Valentino, Gucci, Giorgio Armani, and Missoni. How could six intelligent, talented, and accomplished individuals lose their drive and sink so low? All of them had one thing in common: a devastating setback—an unexpected financial loss, a bitter divorce, an apartment fire that destroyed all possessions, a near-fatal disfiguring car crash—I listened to one sad story after another.

What was most upsetting to these particular men and women about being homeless, I discovered, wasn't the hard surfaces they had to sleep on, or the soup kitchen meals that left a sour taste in their mouths. It was the dehumanizing loss of dignity. This, I concluded, is what had destroyed the will required for them to climb back. But there was still another factor that contributed to their abysmal loss of hope. As the former opera singer explained, "You can live without money but you can't live without plans."

A lack of dignity and absence of plans, I believe, explain the unhappiness of so many older people, including those financially well off. Infirmities,

especially difficulties in walking, hearing, and seeing—
if allowed to dominate a life—make the situation even
worse. One of the most common complaints of the
elderly is the feeling of being useless—or worse yet,
being treated as useless. Congressman Claude Pepper,
formerly chairman of the House Select Committee on
Aging, who lived to be eighty-eight, said, "Ageism is as
odious as racism or sexism."

That's why the gerontologists say it's important for
older people to try and stay fit, to dress nicely, and
to keep abreast of new developments in the world so
they can participate actively in what's going on. Still,
as the homeless opera singer explained, you can't go
on living day after day without plans, or as Elvis Pres-
ley once remarked, "without wanting to do something
worth remembering."

Many elderly entertainers have given us their prescription for avoiding the despair of old age. Bob Hope,
who was still getting laughs at one hundred, said, "It
makes *me* feel good when I make a lot of people in the
audience feel good." Concert pianist Arthur Rubin-
stein scheduled nine concerts in seven weeks when he
was eighty-one. Asked how he had the strength to do
that, he gave his unique prescription: "Eat lobster, eat
a pound of caviar—live! What good are vitamins?"
The indomitable Katharine Hepburn, who lived to be
ninety-six, said, "If you always do what interests you,

at least one person is pleased." And often many more, as one critic claimed she "let her own strength and joy for living flow from the stage to the audience, no matter what the lines or plot asked of her."

Above all, you've got to keep dreaming. Age doesn't lessen the need for inspirational reveries. Robert Louis Stevenson, who once glumly wrote, "Old and young, we are all on our last cruise," was known to conjure up plots by commanding what he called "the brownies of his mind" to furnish him with a story.

I particularly like the limerick composed by nineteenth century poet James Ball Naylor on how old age inspired the highly literate and lecherous father and son, who according to the Old Testament ruled ancient Israel in tandem for a total of eighty years:

King David and King Solomon
Led merry, merry lives,
With many, many lady friends
And many, many wives;
When old age crept over them—
With many, many qualms,
King Solomon wrote the Proverbs
And King David wrote the Psalms.

Inspiration alone without motivation doesn't go very far. As John Gardner wrote: "The self-renewing man is highly motivated. The walls that hem him in as he grows older form the channels of least resistance. If he stays within the channels all is easy. To get out requires some extra drive, enthusiasm or energy." But Gardner also reminds us that as we get older we fear failure and therefore take fewer risks. Nevertheless he advocates trying new things. "Like the jailbird," he says, "we don't know we've been imprisoned until we break out." No need to always keep pursuing old interests. It may be time, as Gardner advocated, "to widen the scope."

Actress Helen Hayes, known in her prime as the "first lady of the stage," widened her scope by pursuing a number of charitable activities after her acting career ended. In her book *Our Best Years*, written at eighty-three, she exulted, "I'm having the best time now! So late? you wonder. The advantage of being at this point in my life is that I neither look back nor forward—I just enjoy now. The trick is to continue to learn, to challenge yourself, and to make some demands on your mind and body."

Widening the scope, I would add, can only be done with a strong sense of optimism. But because optimism is subjective and a state of mind, it's hard to defend as an attainable ally, especially for older people. Nevertheless, I will attempt to do so in the next chapter.

{4}

Sunny Side Up

"Dad, you're an incorrigible optimist," my four sons often chide me. "You're not a realist."

They accuse me of having pipe dreams, of looking at things through rose-colored glasses, or more precisely, through some kind of positive prismatic lens. Whatever it is, they say my sunny views are not to be trusted, that an upbeat attitude can't alter reality, that putting a hopeful spin on things won't necessarily produce the desired result. While they may not be so negative as to agree with the late British psychologist Havelock Ellis, who once declared, "The place where optimism most flourishes is the lunatic asylum," they do think I'm a little loony on the subject of positive thinking. (Anyway, what did Ellis know about human mood swings? He was considered an expert on sex, even though he admitted to being impotent until the age of sixty.)

Still, I try to convince my kids that my unbounded optimism has served me well, catapulting me into a journalism career in China against overwhelming odds. It also helped to keep me from getting killed as a soldier in World War II, and as a correspondent covering Mao's Communist revolution, and the Korean and Vietnam wars. It also spawned a number of book ideas, and even more important, gave me the gall to write them. Physically and psychologically, I feel confident optimism has bolstered my immune system, preventing a recurrence of melanoma following radical surgery thirty-six years ago, and keeping me from surrendering to bone cancer, which I still have, following prostate surgery sixteen years ago.

A pessimistic outlook is often associated with old people. Sure, we can be crotchety and discouraged by future prospects, plagued by aches and pains, or just plain tired of living. A negative state of mind may be so deeply ingrained that some are unable to see the difference between optimism and pessimism—not as clearly, anyway, as the poet, (Elaine) McLandburgh Wilson, who wrote this limerick:

> *Twixt the optimist and pessimist*
> *The difference is droll,*
> *The optimist sees the doughnut*
> *But the pessimist sees the hole.*

Psychologists claim the optimism that keeps your eye focused on the doughnut is an available emotional resource that is ready to be discovered, enhanced, and thereby enjoyed at any age. Yet optimism remains a slippery and elusive subject to discuss because of the mystery surrounding that celestial organ called the brain. Composed of a hundred billion cells (the number of cells does not necessarily recede substantially with age, as was formerly believed), there are unlimited combinations and permutations in that vast circuitry that determine the way we see things. A person has the option of seeing a situation either positively or negatively. "The brain is a democracy," the late Dr. E. Roy John, former director of the Brain Research Laboratory at New York University Medical Center, once told me. "It doesn't listen to a single voice."

Author F. Scott Fitzgerald put it a different way: "The test of a first rate intelligence is the ability to hold two opposed ideas in the mind at the same time and still retain the ability to function. One should, for example, be able to see that things are hopeless and yet be determined to make them otherwise."

At no time is the need for optimism more crucial than in old age. It not only determines your own outlook, but affects how others react to you. Negative and positive attitudes are both rabidly contagious. But we aren't stuck with one or the other. The idea that we can change how we feel by changing how we think dates back to Aristotle, who claimed we experience events as good or bad according to our evaluations of them. Shakespeare echoed the same thought in Hamlet: "There is nothing good or bad, but thinking makes it so." No question, even "septos" and "octos" can train themselves to become more open-minded and achieve a more positive outlook.

Highly successful individuals often speak in various ways of the importance of a positive state of mind without calling it *optimism*. Champion athletes tell of a mystical feeling that shifts them for fleeting moments to a higher level of perception and makes them feel in total control of their game. Earl Woods, Tiger's father, trained his young son to visualize the golf ball dropping into the hole. The Boston Celtics' former basketball star Larry Bird said, "It's scary. When I'm at my best, I can do just about anything, and nobody can stop me." Wayne Gretzky, former hockey great of the Edmonton Oilers, once described what he called "the most uncanny power that enables me to see and play the game several moves ahead of the moment, comprehending not only where everything is, but also where everything will be."

In the same way psychologists claim that a vivid mental picture of ultimate success can help steer an individual to any desired life goal. "No matter how long you live or what you do with yourself in your last years, you'll enjoy them more if you can sustain the illusion of an island up ahead, something to swim toward," wrote Dr. Susan G. Vaughan in her book *Half Empty Half Full: Understanding the Psychological Roots of Optimism.* "You'll spend more time feeling engaged, hopeful, and happy and less time feeling depressed, anxious, and angry." Of course, Americans as a group tend to be innately optimistic. We subscribe to the belief that we have a right not just to pursue happiness, but to be happy, no matter how grim things are.

Dr. Vaughan also claims that "people who volunteer their time and energy to causes they consider worthwhile are often happier and more optimistic." She even advocates faking it if you don't feel optimistic, because as she says, "By acting happier, even if it initially feels fake, you will begin to be happier." In other words, "Fake it till you make it." We can trick ourselves into seeing the island up ahead and feeling optimistic, instead of seeing the future as bleak, as nineteenth century philosopher Juan Montalvo, who also used the island metaphor, did. "Old age," he wrote, "is an island surrounded by death." Unfortunately, that's the way many pessimistic older people feel about their stage in life. They're too depressed even to pretend being otherwise. They seem to feel that their lives ended years earlier, perhaps believing

Dorothy Parker's cruel admonition: "You ought to be one of two things; young or dead," and Stephen Vincent Benet's less brutal poetic snippet:

A stone's a stone
And a tree's a tree,
But what was the sense
Of aging me?
It's no improvement
That I can see.

Of course, coercing the facts to fit an optimistic outlook is dangerous. I recall interviewing Generalissimo Chiang Kai-shek just a week before Mao's armies swept down from the north and conquered the vital industrial province of what was then called Manchuria. Yet, Chiang was still talking victory.

I happened to have dinner with Imelda Marcos just two nights before she and the Philippine president were driven from their homeland by political pressure. She spent most of the evening drawing maps on the tablecloth of all the regions that she claimed still steadfastly supported them—and would keep them in power. However, her optimism perhaps aided her return to the Philippines some years later and her election to congress.

Older people tend to think of their aging bodies as simply wearing out. However, Dr. Deepak Chopra, in his book *Ageless Body, Timeless Mind*, reminds us that our skin replaces itself once a month, our stomach lining every five days, and our liver every six weeks. Then, of course, there is a whole catalogue of human parts, including shoulders, knees, and hips that can be replaced surgically with artificial devices, and many organs, including kidneys, livers, and hearts that can be transplanted. A better and more optimistic view of the human body is as a machine that never becomes completely worn out and obsolete because it contains quite a few constantly renewable parts. "We don't get older," Picasso once remarked, "we get riper."

At the same time, it's important to realize that the human machine does lose a lot of its efficiency with age. For example, an older body generates less power per breath just as an older car gets fewer miles per gallon of gas. Researchers claim that a seventy-five-year-old person must breath three times as much as a twenty-year-old to do the same amount of work. Older bodies, like old tires, also become more brittle. As some wag once observed: "When you're young and fall you bounce; when you're old and fall you break." Doctors who practice biofeedback describe "harnessing the positive thoughts" of their patients to control body changes and eliminate pain. Although some physicians consider that approach to medicine to be just short of sorcery, in many cases it has been proven to help with healing.

Attitude also plays a role in the functioning of the human machine, particularly the mind. Negative feelings of older people about their physical selves become self-fulfilling prophecies ("Everything I eat turns to fat."). In the same way, their thoughts of being unlucky because they are old may actually make them so. Brokers, for instance, claim older people tend to be lousy investors because they zero in on the downside risk of a stock rather than on the upside potential.

It's important to teach predominantly pessimistic individuals, old or young, how to "reframe" the mental picture of whatever they are looking at, to see it in a better light. Remember that clever bit of reframing employed by Ronald Reagan in the first televised 1984 presidential debate? When Walter Mondale, the Democratic candidate, referred to the future president's advanced age, Reagan humorously countered that he wouldn't let Mondale's youth become a campaign issue.

Polite Asians are expert at reframing. Instead of bluntly asking an elder, "How old are you?" the Chinese reframe the question this way: "What is your glorious age?" But then traditionally in Asia, old people are venerated and consulted for their wisdom. The name Lao-tzu, the ancient Chinese mystic and father of Taoism, literally means "Old Master." Legend has it that he was born old, bald with a long white beard.

It wasn't until China's Cultural Revolution, during which the Red Guards launched a mass attack against the aged as well as the intellectuals, that the political leadership became more youthful.

The Chinese are also taught that everything is comprised of a positive (Yang) and a negative (Yin). Perhaps that's why there is no word for crisis in Chinese, but two component characters: *danger* (the Yin) and *opportunity* (the Yang). As history has proven, the Chinese tend to focus optimistically on the opportunity aspect of their problems, which has made them a very resilient people.

Psychologists recognize that older people can be impatient and crotchety, with a tendency to give up after a disappointment. As former Vice President Hubert Humphrey once remarked about the elderly: "They see any setback as the end. They're always looking for the benediction rather than the invocation." But, he added, "You can't quit. That isn't the way our country was built."

Older people also tend to be dictatorial in making requests or giving instructions. A person who shouts, "Don't do that," is less likely to win compliance than the one who says, "Why not try it this way?"—virtually the same admonition framed more diplomatically. The technique of reframing, the psychologists also tell us, can be taught even to old curmudgeons who "see a dark cloud over every silver lining." Reframing is a useful exercise for everyone to practice, not just the doomsayers and doom-seers.

Unlocking your optimism involves honing your sensitivities to watch and listen for things you weren't observing before. "Ever see a master locksmith work?" asks Anthony Robbins in his book *Unlimited Power*. "He plays with the lock, hears things you aren't hearing, sees things you aren't seeing, feels things you aren't feeling, and somehow manages to figure out the entire combination to the safe."

So what does being observant and a good listener have to do with optimism? It imbues the person with the confidence of truly understanding what is going on. ("Nobody tells me what's going on," is a common complaint of many older people. Some even suspect there's a conspiracy to keep them in the dark.) Looking and listening carefully is another way of suspending judgment, staying flexible, and keeping all options open even after you think you've made up your mind. Best of all, it lubricates a relationship, making the other person more interested in what you think and have to say.

"Big people monopolize the listening," it is said. "Little people monopolize the talking." Lao-tzu put it this way, "He who knows does not speak. He who speaks does not know." Mahatma Gandhi said, "Speak only if you can improve on silence." But that's carrying things too far. Good listeners not only hear the words, they get a feeling of what's going on in the other person's world by also paying keen attention to body language and the emotions being expressed.

Gerontologists recommend that older people should try to enter into the minds of younger relatives and friends to better understand them. The key to this kind of bonding is a shared optimism. An upbeat young person may feel uncomfortable associating with an old man or woman who views the world glumly. So it's important for a senior mentor to convey a positive attitude. A few disarming words—"I appreciate," "I respect," "I agree"—immediately improve the receptivity to what you have on your mind. One way to win over the friendship of young people is to convince them how good they are. Remember, a pat on the back is always more welcome than a kick in the ass.

Just as a sunny outlook can improve longevity, fear and worry can cut into it. According to Dr. Steven Austad, a professor of zoology at the University of Idaho, a lot can be learned in this regard—would you believe—from opossums. He discovered that on Sapelo Island off the coast of Georgia, where opossums have existed for hundreds of generations in a predator-free environment, they live half again as long as their cousins on the mainland whose lives are constantly being threatened.

It isn't simply the absence of predators. The answer, the doctor discovered, is hidden in their collagen, the chief constituent of tendons, ligaments, and bones of people as well as animals that grow stiffer with age. As Dr. Austad wryly points out, "That's one of the reasons there are no eighty-year-old gymnasts." After comparing the collagen of the island and mainland opossums, he concluded that the peaceful existence of the island opossums caused a genetic change that made every bone, muscle, and tissue age more slowly. If Dr. Austad is right, people like opossums, who want to stay not just psychologically younger, but spryer as well, would do well to try living in a worry-free environment.

It would be interesting if Dr. Austad could study the collagen of "Los Viejos" (the old ones), as the celebrated long-lived people inhabiting the remote village of Vilcamba in the Ecuadorian Andes are known, or the Hunzukuts from the Karakoram Range in Kashmir, or the Abkhazians from the Republic of Georgia. These people have attracted worldwide attention by claiming life spans of more than one hundred and thirty years. Most proved to be idle boasts because the birth records, if they existed at all, couldn't be verified.

The longest well-documented life span known today belonged to a woman named Jeanne Calmet of France, who incidentally smoked cigarettes all her adult life.

She finally died in 1997 at the age of one hundred and twenty-two. Remarkably, though, her mind as well as her pungent sense of humor remained sharp until the end. Once asked about the effects of aging, she replied, "I've only one wrinkle and I'm sitting on it." Gerontologists believe the maximum possible lifespan of humans today, as well as that of most animals, is roughly six times the number of years from birth to maturity, a figure only slightly exceeded by Madame Calmet.

But more than just living in a tranquil environment, a strong optimistic outlook is usually necessary to attain that kind of longevity. Psychologists claim it's important for older people to keep tapping the same energy sources that fed their youthful enthusiasm. R. Buckminster Fuller, known best for inventing the geodesic dome, became a scientist, historian, poet, mathematician, cartographer, choreographer, and designer all in one eighty-seven-year lifetime. "There's nothing in a caterpillar that tells you it's going to be a butterfly," he once said. "Who knows what a man can become?" But as Dr. Albert Schweitzer, the great humanitarian and winner of the Nobel Prize for his medical missionary work in Africa, warned: "Some people simply let their souls wither. They allow themselves to be dulled by the joys and worries and distractions of life, not realizing that thoughts which earlier meant a great deal to them, had turned into meaningless sounds."

{5}

Tuned to the Immune System

Aches and pains, even at my advanced age, have never sent me to the pharmacy shelves crammed with Advil, Tylenol, Aleve, and the vast array of other nonprescription pills promising quick relief. I see pain as a warning signal of something being wrong, and merely suppressing it with these potions is no cure. Or worse yet, they may even cause collateral damage to the fine-tuning of the human body. It's not just the over-the-counter stuff. I'm even suspicious of the side effects of prescription drugs. I mention this only to explain that most of my adult life I counted heavily on willpower and a positive attitude to help cure whatever ailed me. It's not that I didn't have faith in doctors, or don't accept their advice. But I also have great faith in the healing power generated naturally within the human body.

For the above reasons, as a relatively young man of fifty-four, I did nothing to try to relieve whatever it was that for a few weeks had been making me feel a little woozy. We were living in Hong Kong then, and most of my time was spent flying back and forth to Saigon to cover the Vietnam War for *Time* magazine, not exactly the healthiest commute. "You're under too much strain," my wife Helen said. "What you need is a vacation."

"No, my body chemistry is changing," I kept telling her. I had noticed cold hands and feet, recurrent thirst, morning headaches, and a slight weight loss. For a person who jogged three miles every morning and almost never got sick, I was curious about what might be going on inside me. Possibly diabetes, I concluded. Lying in bed in our apartment in Hong Kong, I kept boring Helen with my symptoms. "Go see a doctor," she'd say and promptly fall asleep.

Finally, the time came for my annual visit to the editorial offices in New York—and the customary annual physical given foreign correspondents by the company doctor. When I stepped on the scales it appeared that I had dropped ten pounds. No wonder my pants felt as if they were falling off as I rushed around New York on various errands. I was just putting on my shirt after the electrocardiogram, followed by the usual back and chest thumpings, when the doctor asked casually, "What about that black spot on your back? Is it new?"

I had first seen the black spot three or four months earlier. I had been swiveling in front of the bathroom mirror to see if I had shaved all the whiskers under my right ear when I caught a glimpse of it, situated below my right shoulder blade near the center of my back. The spot was black, about half the size of a dime. It could have been a birthmark. I asked Helen, "Have I always had that spot?" She didn't know. I didn't either.

"Better have it taken off," the doctor advised, jotting down the name of a dermatologist. The next Monday after a pin prick of Novocaine and thirty seconds stomach-down on a sort of operating couch, I was on my feet again, minus the spot.

"You live in Hong Kong, I see," the dermatologist said. "When are you going back?"

"Friday," I answered.

"We'll rush this through the pathology lab," he said. For some reason that was the first time it sunk in that the little black spot might be malignant.

On Wednesday, I found notes all over the office to call the company doctor. The last message ended: "IMPORTANT—please call him at home tonight." "Well, I must have diabetes after all," was my first thought. Then I remembered the black spot.

"You have a small melanoma," I heard the doctor say that night. Melanoma? Cancer? I didn't ask. The doctor's voice sounded far away, aimed at somebody else's ears, as if I had cut in on a telephone conversation between two strangers.

"The lesion can be excised easily," the voice continued. "There's not much to worry about." I watched my hand scribble the name and address of a surgeon.

A busy round of appointments helped me absorb my bad news. Friday morning I went to see the surgeon, a short bald man who told me to strip and embarked on a meticulous head-to-toe tour of my body. "You have malignant melanoma," he said after I had dressed, speaking calmly and precisely. "Unfortunately, it's the kind of malignancy that does have a propensity to spread. The lesion is in a bad place. The pathology report indicates the melanoma cells are in an invading state." Not a tinge of emotion colored these words.

In a quirk of imagination, the image of cancer cells in an invading state made me think of the North Vietnamese army, pushing south from Hanoi. Were the cancer cells pushing south into my vital organs?

The surgeon picked up a silver ballpoint pent and drew a diagram of the operation he recommended. A circular area about the diameter of a baseball would be excised from my back. "If the melanoma has not metastasized," he said, "you have about an 80 percent chance of complete recovery." Metastasizing, he explained, meant transferring the cancerous attack to some other part of my body—my lungs or liver, perhaps.

"If the melanoma has spread," he continued, coming to the final possibility, "then you're in the Big Leagues."

Big Leagues. A strange choice of metaphor, to be sure. But what astonished me at that instant was not the corny baseball analogy, but that I heard it with the same monotone with which it had been spoken. I felt no fear. No revulsion. No shock. If I had just heard a judge intone my own death sentence, I wouldn't be sitting there so damn serenely! When would the alarm system go off?

"I urge you to obtain another opinion," the surgeon said. He picked up the telephone and called another doctor.

Thirty minutes later, a man with spiky white hair was peering at the lesion on my back through trifocals. He recommended a bigger operation—"radical surgery," he called it, including removal of the lymph gland under my right arm.

I consulted the company doctor. "You decide," I said. "Tell me which surgeon and which operation to have." Then I hurried to catch the Metroliner to Baltimore. I had promised Doug, the second of our four sons, who had a summer job at a tennis camp there, that I would stop in.

As the sleek train slid over the Jersey flatlands, it finally hit me. I was convinced that my clammy hands, headaches, and weight loss came from cancer. I was in the Big Leagues already! A wave of depression washed over me.

That night, I called Helen in Hong Kong, and as simply as possible, described the problem. I urged her to stop off and tour Tokyo with our two youngest sons for a day or two on the way to New York. That way, I figured, she would arrive after the operation was over.

"Semi-private," I discovered checking into New York Hospital, really means "quatri-private." As the new boy in a four-bed ward, I suppose I was lucky to draw a window, especially one commanding a spectacular view of the East River. Watching the boats go by, bound for Long Island Sound, my old seaside stomping grounds, I felt very unsick.

For thirteen years I had lived on the Sound in Connecticut. On this sparkling Sunday, my first impulse was to rush out of the hospital, jump aboard a boat, and head for home. Home? Not from the Big Leagues you don't go home.

· The surgeon interrupted my thoughts. He was the man with the trifocals who had been picked to do the job. We quickly discovered we had both served in the Philippines in World War II. Now he was over seventy and semi-retired. Did he discard the trifocals, I wondered, to do the close-up delicate carving?

The surgeon seemed more interested in rehashing the liberation of Manila than talking about my melanoma, but finally he got to the medical strategy of my operation. "The lymphatic system is the main invasion route of melanoma," he explained. He lifted my pajama top and ran his right index finger across my back, tracing the path his scalpel would cut. His finger dug into my armpit and emerged on the front side of my shoulder where the foot-and-a-half-long incision would end. The ducts, the glands, the whole lymphatic chain from the center of my back to the top of my right forearm, would be removed. "The pathologists will examine the tissue completely," he explained. "They'll thin-slice everything."

Then without warning, he tossed out a cold statistic. "If the melanoma has reached the axillary node under your arm, there's a fifty percent chance it has gone beyond."

Tuesday, Operation Day, turned out to be the easiest day of all. No more surprises. No more options. Nothing to do but relax. An intravenous line was plugged into my left hand, seeping liquid into my body. The operation was starting.

I was staring up at the sweeping second hand of the clock on the white-tiled operating room wall when a sonorous voice from behind said, "I am your anesthesiologist." It was one o'clock—exactly twenty minutes before Helen would be arriving from Tokyo.

A yellow-gloved arm reached out and unhooked the intravenous tube from the needle in my hand. A vial of white liquid was poured directly into the vein, searing my brain. "Count down from five," said the sonorous voice.

"Five, four," I heard myself say.

"You're in the recovery room, Mr. Rowan. Breathe deeply," the female voice rang out cheerfully. Euphoric, that's how I felt. My arms and legs seemed wrapped in electric heating pads, they felt so warm. "What time is it?" I called to a passing nurse.

"Seven-thirty, breathe deeply," she called back.

My right arm was taped to my stomach. But astonishingly I found I didn't hurt. Not anywhere.

The stretcher began to move and soon I was back in my own bed, staring straight up, waiting for something to fill the vertical void. Helen's face suddenly beamed down. "How do you feel?" she asked.

"Fine. Just great."

Told to stand up that night, I felt a steel blade stab my brain—and fainted. But by 6 a.m. I was up walking, pushing a cart laden with bottles and numerous tubes hooked to my body. "You be careful," cautioned a nurse. Careful, hell! I was in a hurry to heal, and to keep my legs from turning to jelly while the rest of my body was mending. If I couldn't run, at least I could walk.

It was the beginning of the four-day Fourth of July weekend, and the surgeon apologized, "We won't get your biopsy back until Monday." *What's the hurry?* I thought. I had to gird myself against cancer on two levels—mind and body. Neither was ready yet to receive the result.

Besides the books, cards, and flowers that came in profusion, little batches of friends arrived at the hospital. They were all wonderful to receive, though sometimes I caught the visitors sneaking a sidelong glance that seemed to ask, "Are you dying, my friend?"

The surgeon had done his work, and well. Now I would do mine. I recalled reading a report that the Menninger Foundation in Topeka, Kansas, had "incontrovertible proof" that some of its patients could control blood circulation and body temperature with will power, literally wishing away such afflictions as migraine headaches. Why not the threat of cancer?

Perhaps I possessed the power within my body to beat the melanoma. I put the question to the company doctor. "Could I build an immunity to melanoma?"

"Possibly," he answered. "There have been cases where even primary lesions have mysteriously disappeared. Yes, there is some evidence that your body could master the disease on its own."

Like everything else in the human body, immunity, I thought, must begin in the mind. First I had to block off any lingering doubts that the melanoma had spread.

Still stuck in my mind, though, was the icy cold statistic the surgeon had tossed my way. "If the melanoma has reached the gland under your arm, there's a fifty percent chance it has gone beyond." Tomorrow, at least, I would get word on the biopsy report.

Lying on my bed watching the sun dance on the East River, I decided that I could, indeed, steel my mind against any further incursion of this thing called melanoma. I could do it no matter how tomorrow's biopsy turned out. I had a simple choice—to spend the rest of my life waiting for the melanoma to strike, or to declare immunity. To believe in immunity, to depend on it, to feel its power. Suddenly I did. I was immune.

Just then the surgeon swept into the ward, his white surgical smock flowing out behind him. Halfway across the room he started to shout. "There is no melanoma in the connecting link! There is no melanoma in the axillary node!"

But I knew it already. I wasn't going to be in the Big Leagues. Not this season.

What also helped me to conquer that cancer was keeping a diary of the entire experience from diagnosis to recovery, as any reporter might be tempted to do. Although during my sixteen-day stay in the hospital, my right arm was still taped to my stomach so I

couldn't move it, I was able hold a stub of a pencil—
the kind used to keep golf scores—between my fingers
and jot notes on a pad pressed against my belly. Then
for the next six weeks, while rebuilding my strength
before returning to Hong Kong, I expanded those
notes into a six-thousand-word article. It described in
detail how I credited my positive outlook with beating
a form of cancer for which the recovery rate back then
was less than fifty percent. *Atlantic Monthly* ran the full
text while *Reader's Digest* published a cut-down version
as its lead story. Several hundred readers responded
with personal letters, exclaiming how the article had
helped them in dealing with one form of cancer or
another. I figured that article closed the books on my
encounter with the disease.

Not so. Twenty years later in 1994, following
prostate surgery, my rear end began to ache when-
ever I sat down. The orthopedist diagnosed the
pain as a strained ligament. But the ache persisted,
and a small shadow on the X-ray finally revealed
the early stages of cancer in the ischium, the bone
inside the left cheek of my bottom. Although the
walnut-shaped prostate gland had been removed, a
tiny tumor left unnoticed in the surrounding shell
had already metastasized. Strangely it didn't seem
at all threatening. Having already been through one
experience with cancer, I was mentally steeled for

this one. *My immune system will surely kick in again and help beat this disease,* I thought.

"You have two options," explained the specialist at Sloane Kettering Memorial Hospital: "Radiation treatments or injections of Lupron, a form of chemo, every three months."

"If I were your father, which would you recommend?" I asked.

"Radiation can cause incontinence, affecting your quality of life," he explained. "On the other hand, you would probably have to continue the injections for the rest of your days." That was sixteen years ago. I opted for the Lupron, and the bone cancer has been in remission ever since. But I'm positive that being tuned in so well to my immune system helped my survival.

Today, a lot more is known about the immune system. The mind, once the province of the philosophers, is now under the scrutiny of the neurologists. They've found that the brain and immune system are connected by hormones, the chemical messengers that drift through the blood transmitting a person's emotional state from one part of the body to another. Like a thermostat, hormones have the power to turn the immune system either up or down. A five-year study in Great Britain of women with breast cancer showed that those who responded to the disease with a "fighting spirit" were much less likely to suffer a recurrence.

The complex set of mechanisms triggered by the mind, the neurologists also discovered, can not only ward off infection, but respond to various agents that cause cancer. Although the effectiveness of the immune system has been found to decrease 30 to 50 percent with age, a lot depends on the individual's state of health, including such factors as nutrition, smoking, and alcohol consumption. But as Dr. Sherwin B. Nuland points out in his book *The Art of Aging*, "The better shape we're in, the less prone we are to get a condition called *immunosenescence*—the senility of the immune system." The root *sen*, he explains, is derived from the Latin *senex*, meaning "old man." And he adds, "No one wants to let his or her immune system become an old man."

Rapid advances have also been made in my treatments. Instead of quarterly injections I now have a tube implanted in my left arm that secretes Lupron for a year before it needs to be replaced. "You're my longest living patient," the doctor remarked this year as he inserted a new tube. "Please don't say that," I told him. "Just say I'm average." Deep down I know that it's my positive attitude and not just that little tube of chemo in my arm that's keeping me alive.

{6}

You and the Eureka Factor

How do you want to spend the rest of your life? That's the number one question facing most older men and women. And it's crucial because you must now reckon with a shorter time span. Perhaps you want to play as much golf or bridge as you can. Or maybe you're eager to follow some artistic pursuit or hobby that you had to give up because it conflicted with your career.

One way to find the answer is to stop being so analytical, the process you are probably used to going through to make major decisions. "Analysis paralysis" is a disease to which older folks are especially vulnerable. Instead, try tuning in more to your gut feelings. The wealth of experience and information accumulated in your subconscious over the years is a reliable resource ready to be dredged up and put to use. If you'll listen to your gut it can stimulate ideas for new artistic pursuits, new hobbies, even for an entirely new career that you had only vaguely considered pursuing years ago.

How does all this work? Psychologists can tell you that the mind organizes past experiences, facts, and relationships into a path that has not been taken before. Somewhere along this uncharted path, intuition compresses a lifetime of learning into an instantaneous flash that I call the Eureka Factor.

It's important for older people, especially those who are still eager for new challenges in their remaining years, to heed, not dismiss, those intuitive flashes. Younger people are usually too frantically busy to give this kind of subconscious creativity a chance to float to the surface. And once it does, they are usually focused too hard on other subjects to pay it any attention. Besides, since intuition comes from some stratum just below the conscious level, it is slippery and elusive to say the least. However, not being able to articulate a hazy, indistinct subliminal message doesn't mean that it surfaced by accident. Or that it was pulled from a void and should be ignored.

Most leaders today—and that includes not just political and corporate leaders but outstanding individuals in the arts and sciences—will admit, if you press them hard enough, that logic and analysis got them only partway down the path to their most important decisions. The last step often required an intuitive leap. Your own experience may have proven this to you. Or perhaps, looking back over the years, you may now recognize that some of the positive moves you failed to make resulted from not having the guts to heed your gut feelings.

This doesn't mean you should jump to conclusions or make off-the-cuff decisions about the things you still hope to accomplish. Reliable gut feelings usually come after serious pondering, even though they may arrive suddenly at a seemingly magical moment. The apocryphal story of how Archimedes figured out whether the crown worn by King Hiero II of Syracuse was made of pure gold or was alloyed with silver illustrates how pondering a decision can pay off. The ancient Greek philosopher was said to be soaking in his bath observing the overflow from his tub, when he suddenly realized that gold is more dense than silver. Therefore a given weight of the pure metal would displace less water. Excited by his discovery he streaked out of this home without his clothes (or so the story goes), shouting, "Eureka, I have found it!" He then demonstrated to the king that his crown displaced more water than an equal weight of pure gold, proving that it indeed was fashioned from an alloy.

This may sound a little crazy, but Michael Hutchinson, author of *The Book of Floating*, advocates resting suspended in a tank or bathtub, à la Archimedes, as the best way of gaining access to the creative right hemisphere of your brain, the side you need for planning new things to do. He claims it is not only useful in weighing the future, but in helping you to remember what it is that made you happy in the past.

An easier, and in my own experience more effective, option than floating is lounging in a comfortable chair and letting your mind wander wherever it wants to take you. "Let go of limited consciousness in favor a much expanded one," Buddhists recommend. In either case, floating or lounging, the important thing is to be receptive to whatever ideas emerge, no matter how challenging they seem. After all, our estimates of human limits are constantly being revised. Remember, the four-minute mile—once considered the ultimate speed limit of the runner—is now routinely broken. In the same way older people are today learning new skills, coming up with new inventions, writing great books, and creating artistic gems, the way only people in their prime were expected to do in the past. In other words, they haven't let the right hemisphere of their brains grow dormant.

Look at the example set by Manhattan abstract painter Carmen Herrera. In 2009 at the age of ninety-four she suddenly became a raging success with museums all over the world vying for her work. Only five years earlier she had sold her first painting. *The Observer* in London called Ms. Herrera the discovery of the decade. "How can we have missed these beautiful compositions?" Her late-in-life success has stunned her in many ways. Her larger works sell for $30,000, and one painting commanded $40,000— sums unimaginable when she was in her eighties. "I have more money now than I ever had in my life," she said. Although she doesn't think of her belated creative success in terms of her right or left brain, she likes to quote a Puerto Rican saying: "*La guagua* (the bus) always comes for those who wait."

Several scientists—Jonas Salk for one, following his discovery of the polio vaccine—have paid special tribute to their right brain source of creativity. Rudyard Kipling also reminded us of his appreciation of the double-barreled brain with which God endowed him when he wrote:

> *Much I owe to the Lands that grew—*
> *More to the Lives that fed—*
> *But most to Allah Who gave me two*
> *Separate sides to my head.*

Most people don't think in terms of what springs from one side of their head or the other. Older people, especially, don't always remember exactly what it was that pointed their career in a one direction or another. Many times they just stumbled intuitively on those life-altering decisions. Both Robert Fulton, inventor of the steamboat, and Samuel Morse, inventor of the tele-graph, started out as artists. From Leonardo's pen flowed magnificent drawing of the first flying machine. Much more recently, from sculptor Ladislas Biro's imagination emerged the ballpoint pen. You don't know what new things you will envision during your mature years.

As the psychologists point out, there are two kinds of vision: what you see with your physical eye and what you see with your mind's eye. Astronaut Edgar Mitchell discovered this distinction when he walked on the moon. From that lofty vantage point he was even more moved by the pessimistic view in his mind's eye—a world badly disrupted by wars, pestilence, starvation, and other ills—than he was by the beauty of our "blue planet." He returned to earth speaking reverently of a "mysteri-ous creative process that works outside conscious aware-ness." He became so convinced that intuitive thinking could best help solve our planet's most difficult chal-lenges that he founded an organization—The Institute of Noetic Sciences—given to that objective.

Of course you don't have to go to the moon to let your mind's eye see all the opportunities that exist for you even late in life. It's possible that some of your loft-iest aspirations may still be achieved. Ronald Reagan saw the White House in his mind's eye at a time most men have retired. At seventy-one he became the oldest man to be sworn in as president of the United States.

Consider also the case of Sidney Harman. An audio equipment pioneer, philanthropist, university professor, and lover of Shakespeare, he purchased *Newsweek* at ninety-two without any previous experience in publishing. Asked why he was willing to take on the burden so late in life of a magazine that had lost almost $30 million the previous year, he quipped, "I think I should stop misspending my youth." Seriously, did he have a plan for saving the magazine? No, but he claimed "there is a plan to be had," indicating that he believes he can come up with one. What seems to intrigue him is the challenge. "By no means do I have a sense that print media is done," he said. "We are at an inflection point among print, mobile, and digital. It is not a challenge to an entrepreneur," he added, "to get on board when the inflection point has passed." His recipe for longevity: "Work, curiosity, humor, and a disciplined diet."

Seeing in your mind's eye the tasks you still want to accomplish gets you only partway there. Psychologists claim it's important to visualize your ultimate success before you start, which perhaps Mr. Harman does. It's the same thing, say, if you decide suddenly to learn to speak French or to play the piano or paint landscapes; try to picture yourself mastering whatever skill it takes.

Certainly, as you get older physical limitations have to be reckoned with. But they can be adjusted to. A doctor stationed at the base camp on Mount Everest reported that a seventy-four-year-old woman made it to within one thousand feet of the summit before turning back. By focusing on your goals ahead, as that woman did, and not on the problems of achieving them, all kinds of possibilities will present themselves. As Muhammad Ali once said: "It isn't the mountains ahead to climb that wear you out. It's the pebble in your shoe."

The brain is wonderful. It has its own guidance system, tuning out distractions and opening up what Aldous Huxley called, "the doors of perception." Or as somebody else once said in describing how the brain focuses on a given challenge: "A hungry man does not hear the leaves rustling." That determined woman climber apparently did not feel the cold or rarefied atmosphere.

If you don't believe that all things are possible at almost any age, sample a few obituaries appearing in your local newspaper. You will be surprised how many fascinating careers first blossomed or continued growing late in life.

Clarence Petty, who lived to be one hundred and four, and could still snowshoe thirty-five miles a day well into his seventies, spent his whole life living in and defending New York State's pristine Adirondack wilderness against real estate developers. First as a park ranger and then as co-founder of the Adirondack Council, he worked ceaselessly to keep the 5.8-million-acre oasis from being nibbled at, building lot by building lot. A Navy pilot in World War II, he also trained hundreds of fledgling flyers how to extinguish forest fires by dumping water on them from a plane. Not until the age of ninety-five did he finally part with his planes.

"Clarence Petty didn't do all this for the thanks," the state's commissioner of environmental conservation said at his memorial service. "He did it for the love of a place he called home for the past hundred and four years." Clarence, himself, had a better explanation. "Not all people feel they need to have a wilderness, but I do," he once told a reporter. "If everything seems to go bad, the best place to go is right into the wilderness and everything is in balance there."

Some intensely active older men and women are embracing their twilight years as a time for adventure. An inner urge seems to be pushing them into the kinds of physical challenges embarked on by people half their age. Charles Smith, an eighty-nine-year-old retired engineer from Delray Beach, Florida, had a hankering to visit the North and South Poles, and came back with photographs to prove he reached both the top and bottom of the world.

An even more bizarre yearning motivated Tom Lackey to take up wing-walking in his eighties. The retired British builder claimed it helped to ease his grief after his wife died. Standing atop the upper wing of a single-engine biplane with leg straps to hold him in place, he flew across the English Channel in 2009 at the age of eighty-nine—and then vowed to complete the roundtrip on his ninetieth birthday. "My family thinks I'm mad," he said. "And I probably am."

Messrs Smith and Lackey may be foolhardy adventurers. But travel agents, long focused on the youth market, are racing to keep up with energetic older folks seeking exciting new experiences. "This is an emerging market," says Ken Dychtwald, a psychologist and expert on the economics of aging. The Grand Circle Corporation in Boston, which specializes in older travelers seeking new adventures, claims this segment of their clientele has risen from 16 percent of their business in 2001 to 50 percent in 2010, while the average customer's age has gone from sixty-two to sixty-eight.

For the past few years while preparing to write this book I've been collecting obituaries appearing in the *New York Times* of people who lived to be one hundred years old or more. As already noted, they comprise the fastest-growing segment of the American population, measured in percentage increases. Here, picked on the basis of their interesting and diverse careers, are capsule histories of a dozen recently deceased centenarians.

Rosa Rio, 107. As an organist in movie houses accompanying silent films, she began her career by improvising sounds to set moods—the footsteps of a cat burglar, the sighs of young lovers, the terrifying roar of the oncoming train as the heroine flailed on the tracks. With the advent of talkies, she became the ubiquitous presence on the radio. Then with the start of television, she played for numerous daytime serials, including *As the World Turns* and the *Today Show*. Known as the "queen of the soaps," her signature piece was "Everything's Coming Up Roses," or as she preferred to call it, "Everything's Coming Up Rosa." In recent years, almost until her death, she again accompanied revivals of silent films in restored movie palaces in Tampa and in several other cities.

Polly Lauder Tunney, 100. A young Carnegie Steel Company heiress who grew up in a world of wealth reaching from Greenwich, Connecticut, to Versailles, she married the world heavyweight boxing champion Gene Tunney after a most unlikely romance. Polly, a striking beauty, met Tunney, a high school dropout, shortly before he won the heavyweight title from Jack Dempsey in a stunning upset. He promised her he'd quit boxing and did after his rematch with Dempsey that became memorable as Tunney's "long-count' victory in 1926. Two years later, when Polly was twenty-one, they were married in a small ceremony in Rome. The *New York Times* reported that the scene after the wedding "looked mighty like a riot as clothes were torn and cameras smashed in a melee of photographers jostling to capture images of the couple." Although Tunney had grown up poor (his father was a longshoreman), he developed a close friendship with George Bernard Shaw and an insatiable appetite for classical literature, especially the works of Shakespeare, on whom he lectured at Yale before he died in 1978. Polly, an accomplished equestrian, sailor, and swimmer, remained vigorous into her nineties, driving a car until she was ninety-three.

Albert Hofmann, 102. This mystical Swiss chemist gave the world LSD, the most powerful psychotropic substance known. He first synthesized the compound lysergic acid diethylamide in 1938, but did not discover its psychopharmacological effects until five years later when he accidentally ingested the substance that became known to the 1960s counterculture as "acid." He called LSD "medicine for the soul," and took it hundreds of times, but regarded it as a powerful and potentially dangerous drug that demanded respect. More important to him than the pleasures of the psychedelic experience was the drug's value as a revelatory aid for contemplating what he saw as humanity's oneness with nature. That perception, which came to Dr. Hofmann almost as a religious epiphany while still a child, directed much of his personal and professional life.

Doris E. Travis, 106. The last of the Ziegfeld Girls, she was a member of the famous chorus line hired by Florenz Ziegfeld, who were as much a part of the Jazz Age as the Stutz Bearcat, the Charleston, and F. Scott Fitzgerald. Beneath towering feathered headdresses, Doris and her compatriots floated across the grand Broadway stages in lavish pageants known as the Ziegfeld Follies, often to the wistful tune that Irving Berlin wrote just for them: "A Pretty Girl Is Like a Melody." Having just finished eighth grade when hired in 1918, she used pseudonyms to avoid problems with the child labor laws. A year later, as understudy for the show's star, she wore a red costume and played the paprika part in the salad dance. She left the Follies to play in silent movies. During the Depression Arthur Murray hired her to teach dancing in Detroit. One student was Henry Ford

II. Another was Paul Travis, a wealthy manufacturer of auto parts. She and Mr. Travis married and moved to Oklahoma where they bred horses, and she belatedly earned both her high school diploma and college degree. In 2007 Oakland University in Michigan awarded her an honorary doctorate. She responded by singing and dancing "Ballin' the Jack," popularized by Lillian Lorraine, a renowned Ziegfeld Follies star.

Sam Dana, 104. The oldest former National Football League player emerged as a celebrity when he was found to be alive, contrary to reports in *Total Football*, the NFL's official record book. It had listed him as having died on July 7, 1969, but identified him as Sam Selemi (his given name that he changed because he said it sounded too much like salami), who played five games as wingback for the American Football League's New York Yankees in 1928. "You can't believe everything you read," he told the *Rochester Democrat and Chronicle* in 2003, when the Buffalo Bills invited him to their training camp to celebrate his hundredth birthday. Belatedly discovered to be the oldest living link to the infancy of the NFL, he was fêted in magazines, films, and newspapers. During interviews he claimed that at Columbia University he had been a teammate of Lou Gehrig, who played football before joining baseball's Yankees.

Eve Curie Labouisse, 102. A journalist and humanitarian, she was best known for the biography of her mother, Marie Curie, who earned the Nobel Prize twice, first in physics in 1903 (shared with her husband Pierre Curie and Henri Becquerel) and again in chemistry in 1911. Mrs. Labouisse's admiring portrait of her mother, from her birth and girlhood in Poland through her education in France to her and her husband's discovery of the radioactive elements radium and polonium, became a best seller, and in 1943 was made into a Hollywood film starring Greer Garson as Marie and Walter Pidgeon as Pierre. In the seventy years since the publication of *Madame Curie*, Mrs. Labouisse was in wide demand as a lecturer. She was also known for her staunch public advocacy of the Free French cause during the Nazis' occupation of France in 1940s. After the war she published the French newspaper *Paris-Press*, and in the early 1950s was a special adviser to the secretary general of NATO. Her other books include *Journey Among Warriors*, a best-selling account of her 40,000-mile trip across a series of war fronts in Africa and Southeast Asia during the 1920s and '30s.

Victor Schreckengost, 101. A distinguished, yet largely unsung industrial designer, he spent most of the twentieth century quietly infusing every corner of the United States with his work, from dinnerware for the average home to the prized Art Deco "Jazz Bowl" for the White House. At his death he was still an emeritus professor of industrial design at the Cleveland Institute of Art, where he served on the faculty for seventy-eight years. While there he designed children's toys, bicycles, pedal cars, flashlights, lawn mowers, fans, patio chairs, golf carts, even artificial limbs. *Crain's Cleveland Business* reported in 2005 that Mr. Schreckengost's impact on the U.S. economy has been estimated at $200 billion. Originally trained as a ceramicist, he was working for a company in Ohio that received an anonymous order for a punch bowl. Mr. Schreckengost made a large bowl glazed in black and vibrant blue, decorated with a Jazz Age New York theme: skyscrapers, neon signs, a champagne bottle, and a tray of cocktails. The client, a woman named Eleanor, liked it, and so did her husband Franklin, then Governor of New York. So they ordered two more, one for their home in Hyde Park and one for the White House, where they were soon to move. From the making of the $50 Jazz bowls, one of which recently sold at auction for $254,000, the designer's fame spread nationwide. In 2006, he was awarded the National Medal of Arts, the country's highest cultural honor.

Jane Sherman, 101. A writer who chronicled the excitement of early American dance, she also lived it as a performer, dancing with companies ranging from modern ballet groups to the Ziegfeld Follies and Rockettes at Radio City Music Hall. However, she was best known as a former member of, and leading authority on, Denishawn, the eclectic company formed by Ruth St. Dennis and Ted Shawn in 1915. From it emerged such modern dance figures as Martha Graham, Doris Humphrey, and Charles Weidman. When Denishawn visited Asia in 1925 and '26, Jane, then seventeen and the youngest member of the troupe, recorded her impressions in a diary and in letters home. These observations served as the basis for *Soaring*, a vivid account of the trip that won the prestigious de la Toro Bueno Prize for dance writing. Believing that Denishawn had become under-appreciated, she went on to write *The Drama of Denishawn Dance* and *Denishawn, the Enduring Influence*. Late in her life she took to writing poetry, some of which commented on aging:

This leathery hen will not call it
a day.
Nor has any intention to do so.
For my wattles are up and I'm
on my way
To as many farewells as
Caruso.

Samuel L. Leonard, 101. A zoologist at Wisconsin and Cornell Universities, his studies of reproductive hormones in animals led to the discovery of in vitro fertilization of women. He was still a doctoral student working with two professors at Wisconsin when they determined that the pituitary gland actually produces two hormones with different effects on the sexual organs. They labeled the first FSH, or follicle-stimulating hormone, and the second LH, or luteinizing hormone, critical in the production of testosterone in men and ovulation in women. When Dr. Leonard and his collaborators published their results in 1931 they created a storm, but other scientists soon reinforced their findings. In the 1960s FSH was used in early experiments with female rabbits to increase the production of their eggs, and in the 1980s with cattle, before being used to develop in vitro fertilization techniques for humans. In his research at Cornell Dr. Leonard worked mostly with laboratory rats, becoming adept at the delicate brain surgery necessary for the removal of their pituitary glands. A colleague recalled his skilled operations in which he could "smoke a cigar, and remove a rat's pituitary in a blue haze, all in about ten minutes."

E. Dorrit Hoffleit, 100. An astronomer at Yale, she studied the features of the roughly 11,700 stars visible to the naked eye and published several editions of *The Bright Star Catalogue.* A supplement list that she also compiled describes their color, brightness, motion, and velocity, and information about how they were discovered. A colleague referred to her catalogue as "the ragged-eared blue book that's always open on an astronomist's desk." Much of her work was conducted at the Maria Mitchell Observatory on Nantucket where she was director from 1957 to 1978. Named for a nineteenth century Vassar professor, it was founded to encourage women to consider careers in astronomy, a mission Dr. Hoffleit supported with a passion. She officially retired in 1975, but continued to expand the star catalogue, helping to prepare the first version that appeared in electronic form. In 1987, the International Astronomical Union named an asteroid after her.

Edgar Wayburn, 103. A physician who joined the Sierra Club to take a burro trip, he went on to lead conservation campaigns that preserved more than a hundred million wild acres. As president for five terms, he also helped transform the Sierra Club from the 3,000-member outing and skiing club he joined in 1939 into a powerful environmental force with 730,000 members today. He was widely respected for the authority he brought to lobbying public officials, always speaking softly in a courtly Georgia accent. "Legislators know that if Dr. Wayburn comes into your office, what might have been inconceivable at the beginning of the conversation, is inevitable by the end," Representative Nancy Pelosi, now Speaker of the House, told *Sierra Magazine* in 1999. As a physician who made house calls, Dr. Wayburn did his environmental work mainly in the evening and on weekends. And he did it without the renown of Sierra Club figures David Brower and photographer Ansel Adams, who were often at odds. In fact, Dr. Wayburn was credited with refereeing their disputes, and keeping the organization from fracturing. But he wasn't shy about expressing his own views. It is said that after receiving the Medal of Freedom, he seized President Clinton's hand in a vise-like grip, and proceeded to tell him of the many wild places his administration failed to protect.

Albert Gordon, 107. After the 1929 crash, he helped pick up the pieces of a shattered Kidder Peabody and built the firm into a powerhouse. He was credited with using his charm on powerful friends like Armand Hammer of Occidental Petroleum and John C. Whitehead, former chairman of Goldman Sachs, to get underwriting business. In a ruling in 1953, Judge Harold R. Medina noted that Mr. Gordon's firm had "forged its way strictly on its merits, from a minor position to one of the country's leading underwriters." He lived to become the "éminence grise" of the financial community, and at the time of his death was the oldest graduate of both Harvard College and the Harvard Business School. Mr. Gordon was chairman and a large shareholder in Kidder when General Electric bought the business. Under GE, the firm floundered and ended up selling most of its assets to the competing Paine-Webber Group in 1994. Mr. Gordon became something of a legend for his dedication to physical fitness, which he believed explained his longevity. He ran marathons in his eighties, often walked from the airport to his hotel, didn't salt his food, and limited his alcohol consumption to one glass of champagne a year.

Reading these mini-obituaries, it's easy to find one common thread running through all their lives—the passion to keep on doing the things that made them so productive during their younger years. Obviously, some inner compass, or subconscious drive propelled them to push on—perhaps not all with the derring-do of wing walker Tom Lackey, or bi-polar traveler Charles Smith, who was determined to go from the top to the bottom of the world—but with sufficient courage not to let old age stand in their way. As Napoleon Bonaparte once said: "Courage is like love; it must have hope for nourishment," and centenarians never seem to stop being hopeful. But then as the Roman philosopher-statesman Cicero also suggested, old people do have a leg up on the younger generation. "The young want to live a long life," he wrote. "The old have lived it." That's certainly true of the centenarians.

{ 7 }

Stay in Touch

One lesson that I learned as a reporter continues to enhance my life as an older person. That's the importance of keeping in touch. It's so easy to lose contact with people, not intentionally, but accidentally, by simply letting friendships lapse. However, the old saying, "out of sight, out of mind," doesn't have to be adhered to. It's pleasant to periodically spend a few nostalgic moments thinking about the people you formerly knew, reliving your experiences with them, and then making contact again.

The network established over a lifetime can be a valuable possession, not to be discarded in your waning years. As the eighteenth century British author Samuel Johnson advised, "A man, Sir, should keep his friendship in a constant repair." This can be done with a note here and a call there. Besides, the urge to communicate with others, sometimes in an intensely personal way, strikes all of us as we get older. And now with Facebook, Twitter and all the other Internet groups, that's easy to do. As Winnie the Pooh said, "You can't stay in your corner of the forest waiting for others to come to you. You have to go to them sometimes."

I have a friend in his late eighties who enjoys testing his memory each night before dropping off to sleep by recalling the names of his former colleagues on the *Wall Street Journal,* and precisely where each one sat in the newsroom. That seems a bit prosaic. He might find it more exciting reviewing the list of girlfriends he had during his bachelor days, or the friends who had the most influence on his career. As Cicero, who commented frequently on old age, said: "A friend is, as it were, a second self." In any case, don't push the delete button in your brain and let the memory of your friends slip away.

There are a few props that can keep this from happening. Hang onto those tattered, outdated address books and calendars (you may need them for the IRS anyway), and don't throw out the old office Rolodex. You never know if any of those former business acquaintances, even one or two you didn't particularly like, are going to suddenly resurface and play an important role in your life.

Two such former friends, who unexpectedly reappeared to help me establish an important connection, immediately come to mind. Both, it so happened, showed up almost magically at a moment when I needed their help.

We've all read how friendships made by soldiers in battle are especially durable. The shared dangers have a bonding effect that can last a lifetime. The same is true of reporters and photographers teamed up to cover a war.

During the civil war in China in the late 1940s, *Life* photographer Jack Birns and I became so close that newspaper ads promoting our stories in the magazine referred to us as the "*Life* twins." We remained friends until Jack died in 2008. *Life* photographer John Dominis and I were paired in the Korean War in 1950, and still are close friends. The same is true of my relationship with photographer David Hume Kennerly. Not only did we cover the waning days of the Vietnam War together, we were among a dozen reporters and photographers selected for an unforgettable visit to North Vietnam in 1973 to see the American prisoners before they were released.

That one-day whirlwind tour of Hanoi was surreal and is still vivid today. There we were, surrounded by bomb craters blasted by our own B-52s, being given a Cook's tour of the city. Next we were treated to beer and lunch at the once-plush French-owned Metropole Hotel. Finally, we were escorted to the infamous

"Hanoi Hilton." When we walked in, the prisoners were standing at attention in front of neatly made-up bunks, as if undergoing a spit-and-polish boot camp inspection back home. None of the prisoners were allowed to speak. A few winks and smirks, nevertheless, got the message across that this was all a sham. Their captors foolishly hoped to convince the world that the horror stories of Americans being starved, tortured, and publicly displayed in tiger cages were being fabricated by the Pentagon.

A year and a half later in July, 1974 when I was recuperating in New York Hospital from my melanoma operation, Kennerly telephoned. He suspected I was feeling a bit depressed. "I want to throw a little dinner party to celebrate your recovery," he said. "And I'll invite Jerry and Betty," as he called the Fords. I assumed he was simply trying to cheer me up. His thoughtfulness on that occasion reminded me of Samuel Taylor Coleridge's observation that "friendship is a sheltering tree."

Even if he was serious I had good reason to believe that the then vice president would never show up. Propped up in bed in the hospital I had been watching the Watergate hearings on TV as Nixon's presidency unraveled.

When my wife and I arrived at Kennerly's little white house in Georgetown on August 2, the street was crawling with Secret Service men. "Could the vice president of the United States, about to be catapulted into the real White House, afford to while away an evening here?" I wondered. Yet when we walked in, there he sat as relaxed as could be, sipping the first of four martinis he would consume that evening. Remarkably, the husky, former University of Michigan football star never appeared to get a buzz on, as much as he might have wanted to. Just the previous day, as it later became known, White House Chief of Staff Alexander Haig had informed him that Nixon planned to resign.

For most of the cocktail hour, I sat with Ford discussing the fact-finding tour of Southeast Asia he was scheduled to make as vice president. We both knew the trip would probably be scrubbed. Yet we carried on this little charade of Ford asking questions about the region's political leaders, while I offered my personal assessments.

A few more friends arrived. We all assumed we were dining at Kennerly's home until he suddenly announced it was time to take off for the Old Angler's Inn in Maryland where he had booked a private room. So, sandwiched between a pair of fuel-injected Chevy four-by-fours crammed with submachine guns and communication equipment, our little convoy of well-lubricated passengers sped off into the Maryland countryside.

At the inn we settled down congenially around one long table. I was seated next to Betty Ford, my wife next to Jerry, a fellow Michigander. This clearly was not a night for serious conversation. David Burnett, known for both his sensitive photography and madcap mimicry, started things off by acting out an argument he had recently witnessed on a train in India. With nary a stammer or stutter, he switched back and forth, imitating the two heavily accented, head-knocking Hindis as they hurled epithets at each other, all the while munching on their chicken tandoori and tossing the bones out the train window.

For the next three hours the jokes and stories never slowed as if a pause might provoke somebody to stupidly ask Ford, "What the hell's going on at the White House?" On August 9, 1974, Gerald Rudolph Ford Jr.—the same seemingly carefree Jerry who was having such a rollicking good time at the Old Angler's Inn just seven days earlier—solemnly took the oath as the thirty-eighth president of the United States.

Three months later, on his first overseas foray as president, Ford came to Asia. As *Time*'s senior correspondent in the Far East I flew up from Hong Kong to Tokyo to join Dave Kennerly, who'd become the official White House photographer, and the Washington press corps covering the president. Soon, much to my surprise, a summons came from Akasaka Palace, the lavish three-hundred-room replica of Versailles where Ford and Henry Kissinger were staying. Ford was still in the bedroom when I arrived, dressing for the formal dinner he was hosting downstairs that night for Emperor Hirohito and Empress Nagako.

Coming from Grand Rapids, famous for its utilitarian furniture, you might have expected him to be awed by the regal trappings of his palace suite with an enormous canopied bed with twin bolsters and a gold damask bedspread that wasn't king-sized. It was emperor-sized. The super fancy surroundings, however, didn't impress Ford, who never seemed impressed with his own importance either.

"It's too bad Betty couldn't come," the president said as he greeted me. Gradually the reason for my visit to the palace emerged. It wasn't to brief him on Premier Kakuei Tanaka's scandal-ridden government, or on any other of the leaders he was scheduled to meet in Asia. He simply wanted to say thanks for my article that I'd sent the First Lady when it was discovered she had breast cancer.

During dinner at the Old Angler's Inn she had lectured me on how all too often cancer patients she knew seemed to surrender to the disease. "Don't worry," I said, "I've been working on an article about the importance of maintaining an upbeat attitude to bolster the immune system. Writing the piece was part of my therapy," I explained. "You lectured me. Now it's my turn to lecture you," I wrote the First Lady in my note accompanying the manuscript.

"Your article helped a lot," said the president. "It gave her a lift just when she needed it." Then we chatted for a while about South Korea, where the president would go next. Suddenly, the entrance to the palace was bathed in floodlights and Ford realized it was time for the Emperor and Empress to arrive. He bolted out of the room and bounded down the red-carpeted stairway. "How'm I doing?" he shouted back to me like a kid who'd just conquered some new skill.

I couldn't help but notice that his slicked-back hair was still wet from the shower and his striped pants were too short, displaying a couple of inches of sock— a sartorial slip the Tokyo newspapers pounced on with merriment the next morning. The local press, nevertheless, appreciated Ford's common man's touch. I did too. I knew then that I wanted to stay friends and keep in touch with this regular guy who just happened to be president of the United States.

My next contact with Ford came in May 1975, and again it was my friendship with Kennerly that brought us together. An American container ship, the *Mayaguez*, had been fired upon and seized by a Cambodian patrol boat. The hijacking at sea occurred just thirteen days after the whole world had witnessed the humiliation of Americans (myself included) being forced to flee Saigon in helicopters from a rooftop near the U.S. Embassy (not on the embassy roof as was mistakenly reported), and from other parts of the city, to U.S. Navy ships lying off the coast.

Ford had responded as if the *Mayaguez* was an American warship that had been captured. He ordered assault troops supported by warships, fighter-bombers, and helicopters to invade the tiny island where it was believed the forty crewmembers of the *Mayaguez* were being held. To prevent a counterstrike he also ordered two bombing raids on the Cambodian mainland.

I flew down to Bangkok, hoping to join the rescue mission, only to find correspondents weren't being allowed to cover the Marine assault. It turned out to be a costly and futile attack. Eighteen Marines were killed. Three helicopters were shot down, and two others damaged. Another twenty-three Air Force security troops, preparing to back up the operation, were killed when their helicopter crashed in Thailand. But the *Mayaguez* crew was not on the island.

Meanwhile, a second Marine unit boarded the abandoned *Mayaguez,* but only after Navy attack planes from the aircraft carrier *Coral Sea* had sunk five Cambodian patrol boats and destroyed seventeen planes on the mainland. Still, there was no sign of the crew, which, as it turned out, had been taken to the mainland. Fearing further attacks, the Cambodians then herded their American captives onto a fishing boat and were ferrying them back to their ship when they were finally intercepted by an American destroyer.

When the *Mayaguez* limped into Singapore, I was there to interview the captain and crew for a late-closing cover story in *Time*. It occurred to me there that the controversial four-day incident could make an exciting book. But to write it I would need both the cooperation of the president and Charlie Miller, the captain of the *Mayaguez*.

Once again I used my Kennerly connection. He happened to be to be breakfasting with the president at Camp David when I called. "Just a moment," he said. "I'll ask him." Ford agreed to let me interview him at the White House. Captain Miller also agreed to let me ride the ship to Manila, a weeklong voyage, to tape detailed interviews with him and his thirty-nine-man crew. But only if I donated half the money from the book to the families of the dead Marines.

After the trip on the *Mayaguez* I flew to Washington to tape the president. Only two others were present during the three-hour session in the Oval Office: Dave Kennerly and Brent Scowcroft, then the president's deputy national security officer. Noticeably absent was Secretary of State Henry Kissinger. Ford made it clear that the *Mayaguez* was his show, that he had followed his own basic instincts to use force, rather than relying on Kissinger's diplomatic designs. Copies of my tapes now reside in the Ford Library in Grand Rapids.

The Four Days of Mayaguez, published by W.W. Norton a month later, cemented my relationship with Ford, who sent me an autographed 11x14-inch photograph of the two of us taken by Kennerly. On the bottom the president wrote: "To Roy Rowan in appreciation of your outstanding work with the *Mayaguez* challenge. Warmest best wishes, Jerry Ford."

Because of my close relationship with Ford, *Time* sent me along on his 1975 visit to the People's Republic of China. Politically it was an important trip for the president. The U.S. election was just a year away and Ford was considered weak in foreign affairs. But Mao Zedong was failing and I could feel the cool reception being given Ford right from the start of the welcoming banquet in the Great Hall of the People in Beijing, which Mao skipped. Ford's abbreviated audience with him finally took place, but not even Kennerly, the official White House photographer, was allowed to be present. If he had been, I'm sure he would have done everything possible to get me in too.

In 1977, a year after Jimmy Carter defeated Ford, I accompanied him on a 5,000-mile teaching and banquet tour around the U.S. sponsored by the American

Enterprise Institute, a Washington think tank for public policy. By that time I had moved back to the U.S., and had switched magazines within the company, joining *Fortune* as a senior writer. My first article, called "Professor Ford Speaks His Mind," involved sitting in on his lectures at a number of universities, to which reporters were barred. One of his favorite topics was what he called "the encroachment of Congress on the prerogatives of the chief executive," a matter still being debated today.

He also consented to spend our flying time in a private jet between stops discussing the issues of the day, as well as his own political future. There was no question in my mind that Ford still yearned to be president again. When we were about to land in Washington at the end of the tour, he started to say, "When I fly back here and see the lights on the Capitol dome, and yes, the lights on the White House, I don't hesitate to admit I get goose bumps." But tears shone in his eyes, and, suddenly choked up, he couldn't finish describing how he felt.

He didn't have to. I knew exactly how he felt, because I was for that moment sharing his sadness. "How did I ever get so close to this former president?" I wondered. It was all due to my friend Dave Kennerly, I knew. Now, more than thirty years later, Dave and I are still friends, and although we live on opposite

coasts, we still keep in touch. As long as he's still shooting pictures and I'm still writing, it wouldn't surprise
me if we tackled some project together once again. As
Alfred Lord Tennyson wrote:

Old age hath yet his honor and his toil.
Death closes all; but something ere the end,
Some work of noble note, may yet be done . . .

By chance, and all because of a similar contact with
a friend, I came to know Ronald Reagan. *Fortune* didn't
ordinarily devote many pages to the pomp and circum-
stance of politics, but it sent me to the capital in 1981
to record in colorful detail the inaugural festivities of
this sportscaster-turned-movie-star-turned-politician.

Sworn in at seventy-one, Reagan proved that some
people's careers, like my own, peak late in life. But
then this Californian had always kept fit, riding horses
and chopping wood at his Rancho del Cielo (Ranch
in the Sky) in Santa Barbara. He looked so young that
a reporter who followed him regularly had once tried
picking a snippet of his hair off the barbershop floor to
see if it was dyed (It wasn't).

Not being one of those reporters, I desperately
needed a Washington guide to cover the inaugura-
tion. Luckily, although I don't remember exactly how,
I latched onto Nancy Clark Reynolds, a lobbyist and

the daughter of a former Idaho senator, who had become the powerful Washington voice of the Bendix Corporation. She also happened to be a close personal friend of the Reagans, so close the family called her "the other Nancy." Still, few Washingtonians knew who she was. It wasn't until the swearing-in of the President on the Capitol steps that their relationship became visible. TV cameras caught the two Nancys sitting side-by-side, the First Lady dressed in red, "the other Nancy" dressed in blue.

Tied to "the other Nancy's" apron strings, so to speak, I was able to crash all the inaugural parties given by the business brass—important for a *Fortune* story— that had been disconnected from the White House for four years during the Carter Administration.

Three months later, when Reagan was shot by would-be assassin John Hinckley Jr., *Fortune* again dispatched me to Washington for an article on the mood of the capital during the tense days while the President convalesced. Nancy Reynolds had moved into the White House temporarily to comfort the distraught First Lady, and shuttled between there and George Washington University Hospital to visit the wounded President.

She told me how shaken she was by the sight of the stricken President lying ashen-faced in his hospital bed. "What sticks in my memory," she said, "is how small and dark the room was. The windows were closed and the shades drawn. Nurses were pounding him on the back to make him cough up phlegm. They had to do that every few minutes to keep his lungs clear and he didn't like it at all. 'That hurts,' he grunted. The public never knew it, but I think things were touch and go." This eyewitness account was especially valuable to me for my article.

Naturally, Nancy Reynolds was there at the White House to greet Reagan on his return from the hospital. "He was in his robe, looking a little wan," she told me, "but joking, joking, joking. On his way from a nap in the Lincoln Bedroom he passed a couple of workmen eating sandwiches in the corridor. 'I didn't know there were any good takeout restaurants in the White House,' cracked the president. He was ebullient, thrilled to be alive and back home. He loved the sunlight streaming through the windows," Nancy said. "'Therapeutic light,' he called it."

While the president was still recuperating, Nancy even slipped me into the family quarters of the White House for a handshake and a quick quote from the President himself.

Reagan's landslide reelection enabled Nancy to keep her access to the White House, though her visits in the second term became more social than political. She began bringing new books to the president's attention. Before Tom Clancy's first novel, *The Hunt for*

Red October, became a best seller she gave him a copy. In nonfiction books she sometimes even underlined pertinent passages.

Unbeknownst to me she gave the president a marked copy of *The Intuitive Manager,* my new book published by Little, Brown in 1986. Only a few paragraphs were devoted to the president, and not all of them were flattering. "That son of Eureka (Illinois) College," I wrote, "tried to beguile America into believing he's just an actor, while actually he is one of the most intuitive politicians ever to occupy the White House—and one of the Eureka Factor's best salesmen" (see chapter six).

I quoted pollster Lou Harris who told me "the amazing thing about Reagan is how unerring his instinct is in knowing when to duck and when to go for the jugular, and how to go for broke communicating it." At the same time, John Sears, the president's former political adviser, had described Reagan to me "as blindly optimistic, fiercely patriotic, and unbending in his loyalty, he is the embodiment of a peculiar American virtue that says all things are possible if you will make them so—that reality is an illusion that can be overcome." (I now like to think that old age is a reality that can be overcome.)

Those brief passages quoting Harris and Sears must have pleased the president, because he picked up the phone and called Nancy. "Hi, this is the intuitive manager in the White House," he said, and asked for my telephone number. Then he called me at the Time & Life Building in New York. I was out to lunch. When I got back our chief operator was having fits. "The president has been trying to reach you," she said, immediately connecting me with the White House. Before I had a chance to grab a pen or flip on the tape recorder that I kept hooked up to my phone to record occasional threatening calls (I was then writing a series on America's top fifty Mafia bosses), Reagan's unmistakable voice was saying, "I received your book and I want to thank you for your very kind words."

I was stunned. If you win the World Series or Super Bowl you could expect a call from the president, but not for writing a book. Besides, I realized Reagan was scheduled to leave the next morning for a summit meeting in Japan, and must have been immersed in various briefings. "You're so nice to call," I said. "I know you're just about to embark for Tokyo, so I really appreciate it."

"With that long trip ahead of me, your book is going to be in my bag," Reagan responded.

"Take care of yourself with all those terrorists out there," I blurted out, still groping for the right words to thank the president.

The entire exchange lasted less than two minutes. But that didn't stop Little, Brown, my publisher, from buying a full page in the *New York Times* Sunday Book Review section to spread the word. The ad pictured *Air Force One*, the president's jet. "The Intuitive Manager in the White House Takes This Book in His Flight Bag," blared the headline, prompting the White House general council to write a letter ordering Little, Brown to "cease and desist using the name of the president of the United States for commercial purposes." The book, nevertheless, became an international best seller, translated into a dozen languages.

Of course, Reagan's surprise call would never have come but for "the other Nancy's" sleight-of-hand—and her Magic Marker. But that was the way Nancy Reynolds got things done, by claiming it was another person's idea. Neither would any of this have happened if I had let my friendship with her lapse, instead of keeping it alive with a quick call here, a note there, and a visit now and then, all of which I enjoyed. For years we kept in touch, even after she moved to Cortez in a remote corner of Colorado to study Indian culture.

Now looking back, I see how much my connections with both Nancy Reynolds and Dave Kennerly helped my career. It wasn't as if I had befriended them to exploit their positions of power. In both cases their help came unexpectedly. As Tennyson also wrote about old age: "Learn to appreciate unexpected small surprises."

{8}

Seeking Solitude

As we grow older in today's frenetic world our need for solitude becomes essential. Solitude soothes stress. It smoothes out the emotional hills and valleys of hope and disappointment. It provides time to evaluate what we have done in the past, and our expectations for the diminished future. It means breaking free from the crowd and convention and finding peace. Near the end of our lives it enables us, hopefully, to look back with nostalgia and not with remorse. "O solitude! Where are the charms that sages have seen in thy face?" wrote William Cowper, the eighteenth century English poet.

Solitude can be found any place depending on your powers of concentration: in a quiet meadow or on a noisy subway; in a hushed church or a crowd-filled stadium; in a solitary room or at a raucous party— provided your mind can just filter out the sounds and other distractions.

As I sped through my fifties and sixties and into my seventies and eighties, jogging remained my main source of solitude. And I continued to run wherever my travels took me, from West Irian Jaya on the western tip of New Guinea, where the men wore nothing but penis gourds and the women walked around barechested, to the bustling sidewalks of New York clogged with gawking tourists. The important thing was not to skip a day. Today, as I look back on all that running, I'm amazed at how disciplined I was.

During the five years (1972 to 1977) I was based in Hong Kong for *Time*, I loved my early-morning runs along a path etched from the rock cliff looking down on the Happy Valley racecourse and the new skyscrapers sprouting up from Wanchai. At dawn, the path was populated by hundreds of Chinese doing their daily Tai Chi exercises. Some of the women brought bits of food to nibble on or thermoses filled with steaming hot tea. A few of the most vigorous young men brought long swords that they waved ceremoniously in the air during their complicated exercise routines. Many of the hobbling old men leaning on canes and crutches brought along caged birds or crickets so these creatures, together with their owners, could also be refreshed by the cool morning air.

While living in Hong Kong I also became interested in Zen Buddhism, partly for the solitude it offered, but also for the power it provided for seeing into one's own being, with what the Zen masters call a "third eye." With such introspection, they claim we can liberate all the energies stored within us, energies that we are not even aware of having.

But the frustrating part of studying Zen is the claim by its masters that words "imprison" or block the very understanding of it. "The more you try to explain Zen the more it runs away from you. It's like clutching for the clouds or trying to catch your shadow," say the experts. "It is something you have to sense, not strive to understand." Having been a striver all my life, pushing hard to accomplish things, trying to achieve what the Buddhists call nirvana (relief from life's pains and problems) in a completely relaxed state of mind goes against my lifelong behavior. Even so, I found that reading Zen poems and stories, particularly *Essays in Zen* by Daisetz T. Suzuki, had a wonderfully calming effect on my mind. And they still do today.

For one short period in Hong Kong I tried meditating, as the Zen followers prescribed, going into a semi-conscious state as I ran along the narrow path. The experiment almost ended disastrously when I found myself about to dive headlong down a precipitous cliff.

During my many months away from Hong Kong covering the war in Vietnam and Cambodia, my morning jogs were confined to the streets of Phnom Penh and Saigon. I loved the fresh smell of the dew-laden dawn in those two cities before exhaust-belching mopeds and motorcycles, buzzing down every thoroughfare like swarms of angry bees, poisoned the air. My route in Phnom Penh took me past a heavily guarded military compound. Sometimes I would hear the click of a carbine being cocked by one of the trigger-happy sentries trying to scare me.

In Saigon, my jogging route took me from the Continental Palace Hotel, where most of us correspondents lived in midtown, to the zoo in the outlying Botanical Gardens. Many of the animals had died from neglect during the war. One tired tiger remained and saluted my arrival each morning with a cavernous yawn. I believe he was as fed up with the war as were the citizens of his beleaguered city.

Back home again in Connecticut, writing for *Fortune* meant that when I wasn't traveling collecting research and interviews, I could work at home, commuting to New York City only on the days my articles went to press. Yet, my appetite for a three- or four-mile morning run, and the solitude it brought, never seemed sated.

A couple of months before my sixtieth birthday a friend and I decided to train together for the New York City Marathon. On weekends we gradually lengthened our practice runs to eighteen or twenty miles. During the race with some 16,000 other contenders, I didn't cross the starting line on the Verrazano Narrows Bridge until ten minutes after the race began. Some four hours and fifty-five minutes later I staggered across the finish line in Central Park, as happy as if I'd beaten the winner, Bill Rogers, whom I figured had taken two steps for every one of mine.

Running continued to be an important daily routine right into my eighties. The kids were gone. So were the hectic magazine-writing assignments. Still, I needed the private time out jogging for philosophic rumination.

On these runs a question raised by the French-born diarist Anaïs Nin got stuck in my mind like a pill can get stuck in your throat. "There is not one big meaning for all, there is only the meaning we each give to our life," she wrote. "What is it?" I kept asking myself as I pounded along on the back roads of Greenwich, "that would give meaning to what is left of my life?"

While that difficult question nagged at my mind, my body faced other challenges. My knees, the weak link in most runners' physiques, were holding up fine. But breathing gradually became harder, finally forcing me to downshift from running to walking, which I still look forward to each day.

Now as a nonagenarian (what an awful word), surf-casting is my greatest source of solitude. A lifelong love of fishing led me to own a series of "stinkpots"(the unkind word used by my sailor friends to describe small motorboats, including the ones I owned for many years), for trolling and tending my lobster pots on Long Island Sound. But boats became a bother to maintain, and today I much prefer casting off a beach. In fact, it was after becoming so smitten by the spiritual aspects of this sport that I wrote the book, *Surfcaster's Quest: Seeking Solitude at the Edge of a Surging Sea*. Fellow fisherman and newsman, Dan Rather, I was pleased to note, called it "an eloquent paean that moves with the increasing rhythm of the tides, and will tug at the heart—and dare one say—at the soul of every fisher-man." Emoting on its pages, I explained how surfcast-ing had become close to a religion for me.

"Our morning devotions," I wrote, "begin at day-break in the great, high-domed cathedral where the faded stars and ghostly glow of last night's moon, are the candles soon to be extinguished. But before the sun's fireball rises out of the sea and sets everything ablaze, we surfcasters breathe in the new day's cool-ness, and contemplate the good fortune that brought us to the ocean's edge."

Experienced surfcasters know there are practi-cal precautions to be taken after such a moment of reverence, and before our ritual begins. Almost mind-lessly we check the grip of our waders on the slippery stones underfoot, open the wire bail of the spinning reel, and whip the long fiberglass rod forward, sending a shiny lure affixed to the free-spooling monofilament off to kiss a wave.

Barely has the lure hit the water when in our mind's eye we can see the silvery flash and flying spray of a striper or blue striking the plug. It's the excitement of a strike that keeps us repeating cast after cast, although deep in our subconscious we know almost every wave is empty—devoid of fish, or at best containing one that has already feasted on so many menhaden and sand eels, its appetite is sated.

Some wag once said, "there's a fine line between fishing and standing on the shore like an idiot." Surf-casting may look that stupid and sedentary to the uninitiated not caught in its spell. But there's a mys-tique to this form of fishing. Standing out there alone at dawn we get intuitive flashes that seem to come out of thin air. But don't ask us surfcasters to explain these sudden realizations about life that come while com-muning with the sea. It's comparable to asking a Zen monk to describe "the sound of one hand clapping."

Occasionally though our contemplations are shat-tered when the sea at the other end of the line explodes. Then the spiritual part of our surfcasting ends and the visceral battle between man (or woman) and fish begins. To be sure, anyone who has never battled a bull striper alone on a beach may not understand the closeness it's possible to feel to a fish. The instinctual strand that can bind a human and an animal doesn't stem simply from the striper's enormous size. Or even from the fight coming from the other end of the line. The connection is more obscure, born out of respect for a creature that had the wariness to elude net, spear, and hook for ten or fifteen years . . . the same instinct that has kept me alive for ninety years.

As we grow older there are many other less strenuous ways to seek solitude in our daily lives. You don't have to "stand on the shore like an idiot." You can sit comfortably at home and meditate. Early every morning (after the fish migrate south) as a few weak rays of light streak the sky's blackness, I plop down in an easy chair with a steaming cup of tea. It seems to warm my brain as well as my hands and stomach, and gets me thinking about my day ahead—and many times about my life ahead. If I'm writing a book, as I am now, and facing its imminent deadline, a little panic may creep into my thoughts, destroying the reverie.

As an old man frequently seeking solitude, my lifestyle has changed in many ways. I try not to rush, allowing extra time for every appointment. I do my best to suppress worry. Epictetus, the ancient Greek philosopher, said, "There is only one way to happiness and that is to cease worrying about things which are beyond the power of our will." Former Teamster boss Jimmy Hoffa once told me when I was traveling around the U.S. with him for an article in *Life*: "Ninety percent of what you worry about never happens. The other ten percent," he added, "is usually easy to take care of." Kidnapped and murdered some years later by his own union members, Jimmy obviously should have worried more about the ten percent that included his own safety.

Actually, I thought he did. A bodyguard usually traveled with us. And when I brought him an advance copy of the magazine with my story, I sat in front of his desk and watched him mouth every word. Finally, lifting his head and eying me coldly, he said: "Just because I've got a gun in the drawer doesn't mean I'd use it." I've thought about that remark many times. But I still don't know what he meant, other than he considered it advisable to keep a weapon within reach.

There are other things I do differently seeking solitude in my old age. Wherever feasible I take trains instead of planes, happy to skip today's airport security hassles, the cramped seats, overbooked flights, frequent cancellations, long delays, and then the enforced starvation even on long non-stop flights. The gourmet meals and body-length sleeperette seats of yesteryears' Pan American Clippers are a faint memory.

Trains, on the other hand, I find mesmerizing: the rumble of the diesel locomotive up ahead, interrupted now and then by the muffled squeal of steel wheels rounding a bend, or by the whoosh of wind from a train whizzing by in the opposite direction. But then I've always been a train buff, and over the years have made a point of riding most of the world-famous trains, both for magazine articles I was writing as well as for the solitude.

The glamorous old Orient Express, the venue for a slew of murder mysteries and spy movies, had morphed into a troop train when I rode it from Paris to Istanbul back in 1949. The Trans-Siberian Express took eight days and made ninety station stops between the Pacific port of Nahodka and Moscow in 1977. That was my longest and most boring ride ever. The train traversed endless sub-arctic taiga forests, interspersed by high-walled, log stockades—the *Gulag Archipelago,* as the formerly imprisoned Russian writer Aleksandr Solzhenitsyn called the chain of Communist slave labor camps spread across Siberia.

Recently, while I was searching for interesting thoughts about growing old and approaching death to be included in this book, a friend sent me this comforting poem by Solzhenitsyn:

*How much easier it is then, how much more receptive
we are to death, when advancing years guide us softly
to our end. Aging thus is in no sense a punishment
from on high, but brings its own blessings and a
warmth of colors all its own. . . . There is even
warmth to be drawn from the waning of your own
strength, compared with the past—just to think how
sturdy I once used to be! You can no longer get through
a whole day's work at a stretch, but how good it is to
slip into the brief oblivion of sleep, and what a gift to
wake once more to the clarity of your second or third
morning of the day. And your spirit can find delight
in limiting your intake of food, in abandoning the
pursuit of novel flavors. You are still of this life, yet
you are rising above the material plane. . . . Growing
old serenely is not a downhill path but an ascent.*

My family and I had opted to make the Trans-
Siberian trip even longer by booking overnight lay-
overs, in Khabarovsk to attend a spectacular circus, in
Irkutsk to watch a marvelous rendition of *Swan Lake*,
and finally in Novosibirsk, where the five of us comprised almost the entire audience in a cavernous opera
house for a performance of *Aida* sung in Russian.

Knowing no better, we had purchased "hard class"
train tickets back in Hong Kong, which meant that
on several legs of the long journey strangers occupied

one of the bunks in each of our two compartments, destroying whatever solitude we might have expected on such an extended journey.

"Hard class" also meant that we were automatically booked into second-class hotels in the three cities we stopped at. Even first class hotels in Siberia left a lot to be desired. Second class meant cots to sleep on and a washbasin to bathe in, with the nearest available toilet either on another floor or in a different building.

That same year, another long rail ride, this one aboard a luxury train called the Indian-Pacific, took me 2,600 miles from Sydney, on the east coast of Australia, to Perth on the west coast. Emus, dingos, and kangaroos took turns racing along outside, while a jazz pianist beat out a little boogie-woogie for passengers gathered around the bar inside the club car. Having been assigned to write an article about this famous train, I obtained permission to ride in the locomotive as we crossed the Nullabor salt desert on what the engineer claimed to be the longest straight-away track in the world. Not a curve for nine hundred miles.

My most unluxurious train trip anywhere was aboard the so-called Reunification Express that crept along at 30 miles per hour over the rickety thousand-mile single-track connecting Saigon in the south with Hanoi in the north. That trip in 1994 took two nights and one day. Leaking windows and the spring monsoons combined to make it an unforgettable journey, especially for my wife, who swore she never would have come had she known she'd be sitting on a wet seat for thirty-eight hours with her shoes in half an inch of water.

But then, unforgettable too, were the stunning vistas as the train sliced through lush green paddy fields and thatched-roof villages, climbed over cliffs high above the South China Sea, skirted the crumbling Citadel and ancient Annamite palaces of Hue, crossed the bomb-cratered landscape of the former DMZ (Demilitarized Zone), before finally entering the capital. It is impossible, though, to make that journey without being constantly reminded of all the young American lives wasted on the war there.

Today, my train travel is confined mainly to unglamorous Amtrak journeys from Greenwich, Connecticut, to Boston or Washington. I usually board the train loaded down with newspapers and books, figuring the hours in transit will provide plenty of time to catch up on my reading. But the train hardly leaves the station when I sink into a semi-comatose state, staring vacantly out the window at the countryside and local stations whizzing by. Not *whizzing by* according to Chinese 250-mile-per-hour bullet-train standards. It's depressing to learn at my stage in life how we are now contracting with the Chinese government to supply the technology and engineers to construct high-speed rail lines in the U.S., with Americans being reduced to supplying the hard labor—the reverse of the situation one hundred and fifty years ago when Chinese workers were imported to lay the track for our first trans-continental line. Today, the loss of vast chunks of the manufacturing sector of our economy to China is hard for me to swallow, having watched steel being manufactured there in primitive backyard furnaces just a generation ago.

Even so, the peace provided riding our own slower trains is precious and I treasure every moment of those rides. Not even boisterous holiday travelers succeed in breaking into my reverie. I identify with the person who Emerson claimed, "in the midst of the crowd keeps with perfect sweetness the independence of solitude."

Sometimes I think we confuse solitude, "the state of being alone," with solace, "the source of relief or consolation," although they are closely intertwined. It often takes the serenity of solitude to find solace. Psychologists claim that solace like solitude is one of our most persistent needs. It dulls pain and reduces psychic stress. Human suffering, they also remind us, is ubiquitous, and solace is the Novocaine that anesthetizes us against the vicissitudes of life right up until the end.

{9}

Looking Back

Not all memories are pleasant. If you are in your nineties I'm sure you probably still carry painful images of the Great Depression with snaking lines of unemployed men and women waiting patiently in front of soup kitchens. And if you lived in New York City, as I did then, you will recall the thousands of destitute families living in packing crates in Central Park. But, at the same time, you probably cherish memories of a more relaxed world that has vanished forever under the impact of television, jet planes, computers, the Internet, fast foods, and most threatening of all, nuclear fission.

Everything wasn't better in the "good old days," but we lived in a simpler and more natural world that was easier to understand. We were also more hopeful about what lay ahead, even though we were no more able to foresee the future than we are now. "Change is the law of life," John F. Kennedy once pontificated. "And those who look only to the past or present are certain to miss the future." That may be true. But I prefer what George Will, the columnist, once wrote: "God gave us memories so we could have roses in the winter."

Dr. Marc E. Agronin, a geriatric psychiatrist, expressed this same thought, referring to what he called our "myopic view of aging." In an article in the *New York Times* he wrote, "We imagine the pains of late-life ailments, but not the joys of new pursuits. We recoil at the losses and loneliness and fail to embrace the wisdom and meaning that only age can bring."

Henry Wadsworth Longfellow also captured that sentiment, as was his way, poetically:

For age is opportunity no less
Than youth itself, though in another dress.
And as the evening twilight fades away
The sky is filled with stars, invisible by day.

Looking back is critical because it forces us to recognize how our lives evolved. Like Longfellow's stars, the important things in life become more visible in the night of old age. We can reevaluate our past experiences from a different perspective. What seemed crucial at the time, later on often seems trivial. And vice versa; what seemed insignificant as it was happening, in retrospect often jumps to the forefront of our minds as a very important occurrence.

While looking back, almost all of us, I believe, can point to one clearly identifiable happening, or one chance meeting, or simply one piece of good luck that shaped our lives more than anything else. I certainly have no difficulty in identifying the single most important and unexpected encounter in my life.

Call it coincidence. Call it clairvoyance. Call it luck. Call it some kind of cosmic connection that even the parapsychologists can't explain. Whatever you call it, there is an inescapable magnetism of fate that sometimes brings two strangers together for a reason. As Daniel Defoe wrote in Robinson Crusoe, "The best of men cannot suspend their fate." In any case, a gentleman whom I happened onto in a bar in Shanghai in December of 1947 would not only shape my career, but steer me to the woman I would eventually marry. Let me explain.

My last assignment as a twenty-five-year-old major during World War II was in command of a reinforced DUKW company based in Manila. The city crackled with sniper fire when we arrived, although the heavy fighting was finished. Hundreds of wrecked Japanese cargo ships, with only a bow or stern sticking up out of the water, dotted the harbor. A few Japanese crew members, refusing to surrender, remained aboard the derelicts. When their food and water ran out they committed hari-kari or hung themselves, their sun-shriveled corpses left swinging from the rigging. Those gruesome images are still vivid sixty-five years later.

Our DUKWs, as the small amphibious landing crafts that run on land or water are called, were busy loading American cargo ships in preparation for the invasion of Japan. Then in early August, 1945, after the two atomic bombs incinerated Hiroshima and Nagasaki, ending the war, my men and I were left sitting around Manila for five months, waiting for a troop transport to carry us home. To make our impatience known to Congress we wrote on the outside of letters mailed home: "No Boats, No Votes."

Finally, marching up the gangplank of the *Marine Swallow* I felt a wave of nostalgia for Asia. I hated to leave that part of the world. Those feelings were partly relieved by what turned out to be a sodden voyage to San Francisco. Liquor, of course, was prohibited on all army transports, but it came aboard hidden in backpacks, laundry bags, and duffels. My twenty-sixth birthday occurred halfway across the Pacific, and the party to mark that occasion went on for two days. We were all ready to call it quits after the first night's festivities. But as the sun's first rays peeked through the porthole, one of my cabinmates pointed out that we had just crossed the International Dateline, and another February 1 was dawning that also had to be celebrated.

My first two months back in New York City turned into a nonstop assault on the newspapers, magazines, and all three wire services, a job-hunting experience that tires me out today just thinking about it. "Send me anywhere," I told a vast array of editors, "though I'd prefer an assignment in China." The last request, I remember, elicited wry smiles and gentle reminders that quite a few returning war correspondents were cooling their heels on dull domestic assignments, eager to go back to Asia.

As a last resort I applied for a copywriting job in the advertising department of Remington Rand. Much to my surprise and, to be truthful, horror, I was immediately hired. The thought of spending years grinding out prose about typewriters was not appealing. But I needed a job.

A few days before starting work I spotted a newspaper article stating that the newly formed United Nations Relief and Rehabilitation Administration was recruiting men and women for work in China and Ethiopia. That night an army buddy from the Philippines and I were trying to drown my sorrows about the Remington Rand job, when we both suddenly decided to send telegrams offering our services to UNRRA.

My thought was that whatever the job in China turned out to be, I could still freelance as an aspiring young journalist.

The next morning, while we were still a little fuzzy from the previous night's alcoholic consumption, a return telegram arrived inviting us both to Washington, D.C., for interviews. UNRRA, apparently, was desperate. Because of my wartime experience with DUKWs ("They're like trucks, aren't they?" said the personnel director), I was immediately offered a job in China as a transportation specialist. So without having done a day's work for Remington Rand, I telephoned the company and resigned. My buddy, an artillery battery commander, was offered an administrative post in Ethiopia, which he turned down. Looking back, I realize there was a lesson learned in accepting a job in China that was not the position I had aspired to. Sometimes settling for an alternative works out beautifully.

After a one-month orientation course in Washington, I found myself in Shanghai in the summer of 1946 serenaded by screams, sirens, blaring radios, firecrackers, and tinkling pedicab bells. As I recall now, it wasn't the stunning contrast of East and West or rich and poor that hit me so hard. I soon became accustomed to the sight of barefoot rickshaws boys padding down the street alongside sleek Rolls Royces, or to starving beggars sprawled on the pavement outside elegant restaurants. It was the inbred corruption that appalled me. Clearly marked crates of our relief supplies were being black-marketed all over town. The Chinese just didn't understand the concept of giving things away free, even to people in dire need.

My stay in Shanghai was short-lived. Tired of my carping about all the black-marketing, my Chinese boss, whom I assumed was on the take, "promoted" me to Regional Transportation Chief in one of the distant interior provinces where I could no longer be a pest. The sputtering civil war between Mao Zedong's Communists and Chiang Kai-shek's Nationalists that was being fought there might as well have been taking place on another planet, for all the people in Shanghai cared.

For the next year another American and I led long truck convoys carrying food, used clothing, and agricultural equipment to the destitute towns and villages caught in the middle of the civil war. Although our four hundred trucks were painted with yellow and black tiger stripes to identify them as non-combatant vehicles, they were continually being commandeered or shot at by either Communist or Nationalist soldiers. In December, 1947, while crossing the no-man's land separating the opposing Chinese armies, a bullet pierced the windshield of our jeep. That did it. We packed our belongings, hopped a train down to Wuhan, and boarded a

Yangtze River steamer bound for Shanghai, where both of us resigned from UNRRA.

Suddenly stranded without a job just before Christmas, and having scored very little success as a freelance writer and photographer, my morale couldn't have sunk much lower. But it did. A rejection letter from the Columbia School of Journalism further dashed my hopes for a career as a foreign correspondent.

I'll never forget my black mood as I headed straight for the Palace Hotel bar. The Palace was one of those Shanghai watering holes boasting of having "the longest bar in the world." Its polished Philippine mahogany surface stretched about one hundred feet from the front of the hotel, facing the Huangpu River, all the way back to the dark wood-paneled lobby—the perfect place to reinforce my resolve to leave China and go home.

"Will you have one?" offered the man standing next to me at the bar, who I noticed was drinking straight vodka that the bartender poured from a tall blue bottle sheathed in ice. "I'm Bill Gray, Time-Life bureau chief in Shanghai," he said introducing himself.

Who would have guessed it? Short and bespectacled, his mien was more that of your friendly corner druggist than dashing foreign correspondent.

During the course of our conversation, I discovered that *Life* just that week had published a picture story of mine that I'd sent on spec to the editorial office in New York. The photos depicted a grisly gallery of five thousand human skulls packed temple to temple on a hillside with ten thousand gaping eye sockets staring into space. This "Stadium of Skulls," as I titled the macabre photographs, had been erected by the citizens of Henyang in Hunan Province as a memorial to their relatives massacred by the Japanese in 1944. Buried in shallow trenches, the fleshless skeletons were exhumed, and the whitened skulls arranged in tiers to simulate a grandstand of ghosts overlooking the scene of their slaughter. Nobody in the Shanghai bureau knew where the story had come from. After we'd cleared up that mystery and downed another vodka, Bill suggested that I stop by his office the next morning.

As soon as I got there it became apparent that he hadn't invited me just to give me a copy of the magazine with my story. He wanted me to write what he called a "situationer," about the headway being made by the Communists in Henan Province where the main East-West and North-South railways crossed, and where I'd spent the last year. "Put in plenty of local color," he advised. "But make sure you've got your facts straight. I don't want *Time*'s editors in New York coming back at me saying, 'What does that do-good relief worker know about covering a war?'"

Evidently, my dire assessment was convincing, even to Editor-in-Chief Henry Luce, a fervent supporter of the Nationalist cause and a close friend of Chiang Kai-shek. *Time* published almost my entire eyewitness account verbatim. I then flew back to New York armed with introductions from Bill to several of the company's editors. No one asked for a resume, or even for me to fill out an employment application. "Are you willing to return to Shanghai immediately?" was all the managing editor of *Life* wanted to know. Unbeknownst to me, the *Life* correspondent in China had just been fired for hanging around Shanghai instead of venturing into the hinterlands where the civil war was being fought.

During the next thirty-five years as I rose through the ranks of Time Inc. covering Mao's revolution as well as other wars, and other parts of the world, and serving as an editor in New York, I never forgot that it was my chance meeting with Bill Gray that made it all happen. But more than that, he in effect became a substitute father for the one who died when I was serving in the Philippines during World War II. In that role he didn't approve of the women I was hanging around with on my visits back to the editorial offices in New York. Without ever saying so, he tried to impress on me the importance of settling down and raising a family, and not just running around raising hell. Finally, he took matters into his own hands and invited Helen Rounds, a charming young *Life* picture researcher, and me out to his home in the suburbs several times, hoping we'd fall in love.

We did. But then I was shipped off to the Bonn bureau to cover the Cold War in Europe. Stupidly, I left Helen behind. It took me six months to realize my mistake. Having now celebrated our fifty-eighth wedding anniversary I have to give thanks to Bill for bringing Helen and me together.

Looking back I think it's important to remember how certain individuals impacted importantly on your life. You may find yourself playing the same role, as I did many years later when we were living in Hong Kong. A young Yale graduate appeared unannounced at the Time-Life bureau looking for a job. He had just finished studying Chinese at a language school in Taiwan. "Sorry, we don't hire local reporters," I explained. "But if you'd like to teach my children Mandarin, I'll hire you myself."

The lessons didn't take, but Helen and I took the young man under our wing, frequently inviting him to dinner, and helping him to get a job with one of the English-language TV stations. And when he returned to the U.S. I helped him get a writing job at Time Inc. where he met the woman he married just as I had. Today, he and his wife live a short distance from us, and their two teenage daughters treat us as their substitute grandparents for the real ones they rarely see in California.

In more recent years I have given career advice to a number of other men and women, and on some occasions used my contacts to help them find a job. It is always a source of vicarious pleasure, though I'm aware of what the seventeenth century French writer, Francois, Duc de la Rochefoucauld, once claimed: "Old people like to give good advice as solace for no longer being able to provide bad examples."

Although Henry Luce was far from the father figure of Bill Gray, it could be argued that he was really the key person in my life. Both intimidating and aloof around the office (choosing, for example, to ride the elevator alone to the thirty-fourth floor so he didn't have to make small talk with the employees), he could be warm and friendly to his correspondents out in the field. Without his approval I never would have been hired by *Life*. And my eventual friendship with him certainly helped to advance my career on his three most important magazines, *Life*, *Time*, and *Fortune*.

My first encounter with Harry, as we all called him, came early in 1949 when he summoned me from Shanghai—some ten thousand miles away—just for lunch. He was hoping that I'd be able to tell him that things weren't going as badly as they appeared for his good friend Chiang Kai-shek in his battle to save China from the Communists. Flying back to New York I was reminded that two of my predecessors, Teddy White and John Hersey, had lost their jobs telling Harry the truth about Chiang's corrupt regime.

As Luce entered the private dining room he greeted me with a paternal pat on the shoulder, as if to confirm that I had done all right in my first year on *Life* and he was glad to have me in the Time Inc. family.

As the lunch progressed he showed himself to be a man of contradictions. He was shy but candid. He was very opinionated, but he was also consumed with curiosity. One moment he sounded controlled and cold, the next moment he was full of boyish enthusiasms. He was bright all right. But as his mind darted and jumped, several ideas seemed to be trying to escape from his mouth at one time, causing a slight stammer.

After I delivered a dismal appraisal of the war, he dwelled on happier days when he was a "mishkid," as the sons and daughters of American missionaries in China were called. He described the avid fund-raising for Yenching University that his father had done. Yes, he had until recently still retained hope that Chiang would prevail. He had put pressure on Truman, he said, to send more military and economic aid. He'd also searched for splits within the Guomindang Party that might have spawned a more populist movement in China to resist the fast-running Red tide.

Suddenly ending this soliloquy, the editor-in-chief started firing questions at me. "Will Mao's troops have to regroup before sweeping south?" "How long can Nanjing and Shanghai hold out?" "Will a wave of panic hit those cities before the Communists move in?"

Luce's reputation for being a relentless questioner was legendary among his foreign staff. Once on the way in from the airport in Paris he discombobulated *Time*'s bureau chief by asking him to identify every structure on the way. Passing an excavation for a new building, Luce said, "And what's that?"

"It's a hole in the ground, Harry," blurted the exasperated bureau chief.

As Luce continued to pepper me with more questions, I noticed how he cocked his head slightly to the left, weighing each answer. He was a good listener. I wondered whether William Randolph Hearst or Colonel Robert McCormick, or any of the other publishing giants with his immense power and influence, would have been so receptive to the ideas of a lowly reporter.

At the end of the lunch I was surprised how pained Luce looked when I told him that not only was Chiang on the brink of defeat, but that the Time-Life bureau would probably have to be moved to Hong Kong, out of the country where he'd been born, had grown up, and had loved. The thought of not being able to visit China again appeared to cause him great anguish.

It was unusual to be called in from the field like that to meet with Harry, because he took special pleasure in visiting the bureaus. During his wife Clare Boothe Luce's appointment as ambassador to Italy in 1953, he apparently didn't like playing second fiddle, or as *Time*'s Rome correspondent put it, "being a State Department dependant," so he went bureau-hopping all over Europe.

When he showed up in Bonn I was away in Yugoslavia covering a Partisan rally for Marshal Tito, and Helen filled in as his date. A bureau picnic was arranged down in the Ahr Valley, famous for its red wine. "Germans don't drink wine," Harry insisted to Helen. "They drink beer!" She didn't argue, but diplomatically sent one of the bureau drivers speeding off to a neighboring village to pick up a case of Beck's. That little episode reminded me of a remark by the nineteenth century American humorist, Josh Billings: "The trouble with people is not that they don't know, but they know so much that ain't so."

Luce, however, didn't often get caught making false claims. A keen observer of people and events, his memos to staff members were both precise and incisive, setting an example for his reporters and editors.

Being a good reporter himself, I believe, had a lot to do with the success of the company he created.

On another visit by Luce to the Bonn bureau that same year, I was in the midst of planning a special issue of *Life*, devoted entirely to post-war Germany. It was a mammoth project, consuming all of my time and energy for the previous two months.

I took Luce to lunch at the Adler Hotel, known for its venison smothered in a delicious cherry sauce, an entree that I recommended highly. Luce ordered a steak, getting our lunch off on a slightly discordant note. Then for the next hour he poured out enough story ideas to fill two special issues. Usually a good listener, on this occasion he paused only when his lifelong stammer interrupted the flow of words. I became so exasperated that when he left to go to the men's room, I followed him in. "Now's my chance," I thought as he stood facing the urinal with his back to me. But as I started to speak, he raised his right arm for silence. Today, it appalls me to think I wasn't going to let the poor man pee in peace.

Fortunately, most all of my subsequent dealings with Luce were more successful. Several years later as the assistant managing editor of *Life* I produced a couple of special issues, one on the hundred most influential Americans under the age of forty that I called "The Takeover Generation." "Your special issue,"

Luce scribbled in a flattering handwritten note to me, "is one that I'm proud to have published."

But then Luce created a corporate culture in which editors, writers, and reporters became part of his extended family and were encouraged to spend their entire careers at Time Inc.—quite different from the situation today when a man or woman starting out in business can expect to have six or seven employers before retiring. He did, however, believe in switching people between magazines, believing that the cross-fertilization strengthened his publications.

But as influential as Luce was on *my* life, it is still clear looking back that Bill Gray was the one person who controlled my destiny the most. One of my deepest regrets is that I never got to thank him before he died suddenly of heart failure at the age of fifty-four. His twin sister lived to be almost one hundred, proving that the gene pool in one family is not always fairly apportioned.

So, Bill, one last time with feeling: "*Amicitiae nostrae memoriam spero sempiternam fore*," as Cicero wrote. "I hope the memory of our friendship will be everlasting."

{10}

Looking Ahead

"Go forth to meet the shadowy future, without fear, and with a manly heart," wrote the poet Henry Wadsworth Longfellow. That's easier said than done. The future is so "shadowy" and unpredictable that many of us in our later years look ahead with great trepidation. Old age can loom up as a sea of boredom, if not a period of considerable physical pain. But it doesn't have to be so. If you are still in reasonably good health, and have a career or set of interests to pursue, the swan song years can be among your most productive. But as the British essayist Clive Staples Lewis pointed out, no matter how you envision spending the years ahead, "The future is something everybody reaches at the rate of sixty minutes an hour, whatever he does, whoever he is." Or as the renowned American inventor, Charles Kettering, wrote, "We should all be concerned about the future because we will have to spend the rest of our lives there."

Most encouraging, it is now recognized that new powers of the mind can be developed late in life— including the ability to concentrate, meditate, and to expand awareness and consciousness. As Robert Butler, former head of the National Institute on Aging, wrote: "We rarely find anyone paying attention to the growth of wisdom in the individual with age." Yet, he and other experts nevertheless claim they wouldn't be surprised if the wisdom of elders turned out to be "biologically based," and "not just polite recognition of the past services rendered." In any case, wisdom comes from a life of effort. As Abigail Adams wrote in a letter of encouragement to her depressed husband, President John Adams: "Wisdom is the fruit of experience, not the lesson of retirement and leisure."

Even if you aren't so energetically endowed with a career that can be continued, this can be a time to develop new interests. As has been frequently suggested, learn to play a musical instrument, master a foreign language, take up sketching or painting, or enroll in a course in gourmet cooking. Or if none of those activities are appealing, there are libraries full of books to read, an activity that can be especially comforting for those who are lonely. As the nineteenth century philosopher Martin Farquhar Tupper wrote, "A good book is the best of friends, the same today and forever."

Given sufficient thought, books can also spawn new personal objectives, or belatedly a whole new perspective on life. But then as eighteenth century statesman Edmund Burke claimed: "To read without reflecting, is like eating without digesting."

Experts on aging claim that most people, in fact, seem to become happier, even healthier, after retirement—especially those who didn't care that much about their jobs. Attitude is the key, since the opportunities open to older people are indeed mainly limited by what the individual is determined to achieve. A person in retirement has more time to take care of himself, to eat and exercise properly, to get enough rest, and to work productively in some less competitive way. Some men and women even find themselves working harder in retirement than they did before, mainly because they enjoy it. Mark Twain, who relished writing, used to insist that he never worked, only played.

But then any new pursuit takes courage. I suspect it's more the fear of failure than lethargy that keeps most of us older folks from trying to acquire new skills. "Behold the tortoise," wrote James Bryant Conant, the former president of Harvard University. "He only makes progress when he sticks his neck out." So go ahead and take a chance on whatever it is you want to do.

Speaking of tortoises, the gerontologists are fascinated with the Galapagos tortoises. These huge lumbering creatures go on enjoying life for one hundred and fifty years. Perhaps the secret hidden in their DNA (the double-helix molecule that is our heritage messenger) will someday teach us humans how to extend our own lives for another fifty or sixty years. But as of now gerontologists take the dim view that old age is just another disease that every human eventually gets and dies from.

If it's a disease, does it necessarily follow that the ultimate human life span has been extended by modern medicine? "Surprisingly it hasn't," claims Albert Rosenfeld, one of my former colleagues at *Life*, in his fascinating book *Prolongevity II.* "What has been extended is our average life expectancy" (Now 80.4 years for American women, and 75.3 for men, according to the National Center for Health Statistics).

As Rosenfeld's book points out, in the age of Pericles the average life span was only about twenty-two because of the high rate of infant mortality, and all the diseases considered incurable then. But some individuals did live to the same ripe old age that people do today. Only they weren't shunted off to assisted living establishments, but rather were among the elite elder statesmen, artists, and poets whose wisdom and skills were revered.

Sophocles, for example, wrote *Oedipus Rex* when he was seventy-five and finished writing *Oedipus at Colonus* at eighty-nine, just a year before his death. And

according to Rosenfeld, "he didn't need the equiva-
lent of Masters and Johnson to tell him that men of
his age were still sexually effective." In Sophocles' final
years two young women, Theoris and then Archippe,
helped "to keep his bones and bed warm." Theoris
even made Sophocles a father again, enraging his
legitimate son, Iophon, who, suspecting he might be
disinherited, tried to have his father declared incom-
petent. But Sophocles convinced the court he was of
sound mind.

Most of us in sound mind aspire to live to a ripe
old age. Today hundredth birthdays are commonplace. But it's not just that people are living longer—
the important thing is they are staying active longer,
according to Dr. Gary Kennedy, director of geriatric
psychiatry at the Montefiore Medical Center in New
York. A strong survival instinct plus a desire to keep
on tasting all the pleasures the world has to offer is
what keeps most of us going. And to that end the
medical profession is cooperating very successfully by
making available a vast array of miracle drugs, and a
thick catalog of spare parts, including artificial knees,
shoulders, and limbs and transplanted livers, kidneys,
heart valves (most from pigs and calves), and in a few
instances whole beating hearts. But those new pro-
cedures can only keep the body active. Keeping the
mind active is the responsibility of each individual.

Even after surviving two serious bouts of cancer, I
know what is propelling me deeper into my nineties,
and happily so. It's not the little glass tube inserted in
my left arm that seeps a chemo drug called Lupron
into my bloodstream, only to be replaced with another
tube after a year. It's my fervent desire to keep on living life to the fullest and to complete certain things I
started years ago. In fact, it's not a bad idea to pur-
posely save some projects and new pursuits for your
retirement years, when you aren't bogged down with
raising a family or a full-time job or climbing the corporate ladder to a loftier position. But that takes considerable advance planning.

"Most of those who fail to thrive in retirement,"
Rosenfeld claims, "do not of course commit suicide;
they simply go downhill fairly rapidly. The tragedy is
avoidable, or would have been, with some thought and
preparation."

Why is it so important to make advance plans for
retirement? Because without them you may feel like a
lost soul once you've ended your full-time employment.
Dr. Jerome Frank of Johns Hopkins, in his book, *Per-
suasion and Healing*, describes how in a northern Austra-
lian tribe, the Murgin, when the death of a man's soul
becomes generally known, he and his fellow tribesmen
collaborate in hastening his demise, and conduct pre-
mature mourning ceremonies.

Dr. Frank equates retirement ceremonies with mourning ceremonies. "When we force a still-vigorous individual to retire, do we not in a sense steal his soul?" he asks. "The more fool he, of course, for having permitted his employment to *become* his soul, to be so easily stolen."

When I returned from China at the end of the civil war there in 1949, an editor at Little, Brown dangled a fat book contract in front of me. "Okay, you need some time off to digest your thoughts," he said. "Then sit down and write an eyewitness account of the last three years of the Communist revolution." He claimed the book could advance my career as a journalist the same way *Thunder Out of China* did for Teddy White. "Your story begins where Teddy's left off," he said. "You are one of few Americans who covered the final chapter of Mao's rise to power."

But, the thought of even temporarily interrupting my own rise through the ranks at *Life* was not appealing. The magazine had already ticketed me for a plush assignment covering the special Holy Year events in Rome, an assignment that was quickly changed to covering the war in Korea when fighting broke out between the North and South in 1950. The China memoir that the Little, Brown editor suggested, I thought, would be a good project for some time in the future. And it was.

{11}

Recycling the Past

In 2003 an editor at the Lyons Press called. "Why don't you look through your old China notes and articles," he said, "and see if there isn't a fascinating memoir there."

At first I was turned off by the thought of rehashing old adventures. Fortunately I had kept all of my old notes as well as hundreds of photographs. Several times Helen had urged me to get rid of all the dusty old cartons of carbon copies of files I'd hammered out on the Olivetti that I carried with me in China between 1946 and 1949. As I started sifting through the hundreds of frayed onionskin pages, a few crumbled in my fingers. But the adventures described on those tattered pages sprang to life again.

The sights, the sounds, the sensations, all came flooding back. It was if I had returned to China's Central Plain and was once again escorting United Nations truck convoys carrying relief supplies to the devastated towns and villages in the so-called Flooded Area south of the Yellow River. Chiang Kai-shek had blown the dikes there intentionally during World War II in a futile attempt to stop the Japanese invasion. But the dikes were being repaired and half a million farmers, driving mule carts, pushing wheelbarrows, or simply carrying all their belongings on their backs, were returning to reclaim their land.

I was surprised how vivid my untutored writing was back then. In the frayed old files I found descriptions such as the following about the difficulty of simply driving a motor vehicle over China's ancient roads that I could never have recreated out of memory:

For the first few months I had driven cautiously, easing my jeep gingerly in and out of craters and humps. Patience and care gradually gave way to masochism. Now I stomped the accelerator, holding tight to the steering wheel as the jeep smashed into holes or took off into the air. The windshield might crack, the springs might snap, and the radiator needed resoldering after every trip. Still the engine kept whining angrily while I sucked in mouthfuls of red dust and cursed every jolt. Lurking in the back of my mind was the hope with the next solid whack my battered jeep might finally lay down and die. Then I could walk as was intended on these ancient roads of China.

Many of the tattered pages were devoted to my anger at delivering food, clothing, agricultural equipment, and other supplies to warehouses controlled by the corrupt provincial officials, who then sold the stuff to black-marketeers instead of distributing it to the impoverished farmers. But most of my frustrations concerned being caught in the shifting tides of the civil war. Towns and villages kept changing hands. One week a town in this contested area would be occupied by Chiang Kai-shek's Nationalists, the next week by Mao's Communists.

If the military situation hadn't been so tragic in the town of Fukou my old description below of the ridiculous way it kept changing hands might have been taken from a scene in a Chinese comic opera.

Fukou had been badly damaged by both armies. Hit first by Communist artillery shells and then by Nationalist dive-bombers, a gaping hole had been blown in the outer wall, making it easy for either of the invading armies to enter. Living in an age that already knew the destructive power of an atomic bomb, I hadn't appreciated the protection afforded by a mud wall forty feet high and twenty feet thick in repelling infantry attacks.

I soon discovered that the sudden policy changes implemented every time Fukou changed hands caused as much havoc as the soldiers.

When the Communists first captured Fukou they published a roster of the richest families whose houses could be ransacked by all comers in an informal wealth equalization program. Only removable items, it was expected, would be taken. But after hundreds of spirited looters had cleaned out the porcelain ware, furniture, and other valuables, they took to unhinging doors, prying out window frames, and peeling wood panels from the walls. So the Communists finally called a halt to the proceedings. When a few latecomers arrived and started chipping out bricks and removing roof tiles, they were hauled off to the dike and shot.

The next week the Nationalists returned. "Since when had looting been legalized?" they wanted to know. An order was issued to return all the stolen items. And to make sure everyone understood, a dozen of the worst offenders were escorted out to the same dike and shot through the head. But the Nationalist authorities failed to mention where the loot was to be returned. When the sun came up the next morning, the stuff was scattered through the streets.

Rereading those old files, I was pleasantly surprised not only by the quality of the writing, but by the amount of detail I'd absorbed. My professional journalistic experience had been limited to two low-paying college stringerships. During my senior year at Dartmouth the *Boston Post* had paid me twenty-five cents a column inch, and for copies of the same stories, the *Springfield Republican* paid me another fifteen cents an inch. At Dartmouth's football games I sat in the press box with a Western Union telegrapher at my side, tapping out my play-by-reports in Morse code simultaneously to both newspapers.

While working for UNRRA most of my writing consisted of scribbled vignettes that I hoped to combine into full-blown freelance articles. An agent friend in New York said she would try to sell the articles for me, but she wasn't optimistic. Photos, yes, she could probably find a market for those. However, it never occurred to me then that the voluminous notes I was taking would someday become fodder for a book.

My first chance for an important story came unexpectedly in 1947 when I was still in Kaifeng, Henan's teeming provincial capital where my truck depot was located. I remember the day began like every other, as my notes below described:

A long line of men, women, children, oxen, mules, dogs, chickens, pigs, and sheep stood quietly outside the city wall, waiting for daybreak when the soldiers ordinarily opened the heavy spiked iron gate so they could proceed inside to sell their goods. But on this day the gate remained closed.

At the railway station the waiting scene was being repeated. Streaks of light were beginning to show in the sky above the weary travelers sprawled out on the platform beside their belongings. As they commenced to stir, young girls carrying kettles of water and cakes of soap in brass basins circulated through the crowd charging 500 Yuan (one cent) a wash. But the rail yard behind the station remained quiet except for the shouts of a few naked soot-smeared children pitifully picking through the stones and ashes for pieces of coal for their mothers to sell.

The eastbound express arriving from Xian and proceeding on to Xuzhou, Nanjing, and Shanghai hadn't appeared for two days, and it wouldn't again today, the stationmaster announced, although nobody knew why. Most likely the Communists had dynamited the tracks somewhere up the line.

The city center was also just coming awake. Shopkeepers on Sheng Fu Lu (Provincial Government Street) had begun to peel the protective board panels from their display windows. The "honey cart" men were already out collecting wheelbarrows full of pungent human excrement for delivery to the outlying farms. A few rickshaw boys padded noiselessly up and down the street pulling early morning fares. Others stood in the shafts of their empty rickshaws slurping noodles from crockery bowls.

A boy suddenly raced down the street chattering excitedly to the baffled rickshaw boys and shopkeepers: "The soldiers are coming! The soldiers are coming!" Soon soldiers swarmed down Sheng Fu Lu and the traffic stopped. The shopkeepers hurriedly put back the boards on their windows, and the pedestrians, rickshaws, carts, and animals were herded into the alleys and side streets.

Rumors flew. "The one-eyed Liu Bo-cheng, commander of the Communist Eighth Route Army, is attacking from the north." "General Chang Shao-hua has broken out of the Flooded Area and is attacking from the south." "The Yellow River dikes have been blown and Kaifeng will soon be flooded." Something truly bad must be happening. Then a strange sight dispelled everyone's worst fears.

My description ended there. But I remember how platoons of coolies, carrying shovels over their shoulders, quickly dispersed and started filling in the deep ruts and leveling off the bumps in the road.

"Amazing!" I thought. "The streets hadn't been repaired for years." But the bamboo telegraph worked fast in Kaifeng, and a fresh rumor swept the city: "The Generalissimo is coming."

That rumor caught hold, and apparently my interest did too, because my notes resumed:

Shopkeepers quickly splashed whitewash on their storefronts and swept their walks. Women hurriedly dressed children ordinarily allowed to run naked through the streets. Overhead the air suddenly droned with the sound of P-51 fighter planes circling the city.

Soon an olive-colored C-47 hovered over Kaifeng and quickly set down on the concrete airstrip left by the Japanese. A few minutes later, a motorcade of armed trucks and dilapidated official cars roared down Sheng Fu Lu, followed by a shiny black limousine. As it sped by I glimpsed the bald-headed Generalissimo sitting erect in the back seat.

This man, I recalled thinking, was no comic opera general like the one portrayed by Communist placards. He was one of the world's Big Five, the Chinese leader who had dared challenge the Asian military strategy of Winston Churchill and Franklin Roosevelt during World War II, passing right in front of me. And without another reporter within five hundred miles, or a telegrapher at my side to send my story.

Chiang's appearance, I realized, meant that the Nationalist military situation in the strategic rail hub of Kaifeng, once the capital of all China, had become desperate, just as I had suspected from the recent flurry of Communist attacks on my truck convoys. Obviously, the Generalissimo had come to stiffen the backbone of his generals, famous for avoiding combat, and even worse, for selling their soldiers' weapons to the Communists.

Brigadier General Zhou Enlai, Mao's deputy, had made several secret visits to Kaifeng, and I had met him briefly once, but only because of his complaint that the Communist-held towns weren't receiving their fair share of the relief supplies being transported by my trucks. But the Generalissimo rarely ventured this far into the interior.

I still remember how steaming mad I was at having no way to telegraph my scoop to Shanghai, or that no news organization was there to disseminate it. However, I was seeing first hand one of Chiang's feeble responses to Mao's military strategy of infiltrating the countryside and cutting off the cities until they fell of their own weight like ripe melons.

For the next two years, as an accredited correspondent for *Life*, my situation was different. My eyewitness reports had a magazine to go in. And the voluminous files I wrote then were easy to assemble for use in writing the book the editor at the Lyons Press suggested.

Today, quite a few of my friends are doing practically the same thing—delving into their old letters, files, and photo albums to write a family history, not to sell as a book, but as a record for succeeding generations. It's a time-consuming job that can take years. But carried along on waves of nostalgia it can be an enlightening and entertaining post-retirement project. And now with computers, digital cameras, and electronic scanning equipment, turning the results into a privately printed book can be easily and inexpensively done.

Minus such technology *Life* photographer Jack Birns and I had to ship his undeveloped rolls of film by plane to New York and send my accompanying captions and stories by cable. As for phone service to the interior, you might as well have tried to call Mars. So the only way to find out where the battles were being fought was by hitching rides on military supply planes all over China. That way we covered the fall of all the major cities, from Mukden, the highly industrialized capital of Manchuria in the north, down to the Communist takeover of Shanghai, China's beating commercial heart.

We were in Beijing when Chiang's trusted defender, General Fu Zuoyi, defected and peacefully handed the city over to the Communists, and then switched sides, becoming Mao's minister of forestry. Several weeks later, flying into Taiyuan, the Nationalists' main arsenal, we found it surrounded, and being bombarded around the clock by Communist artillery. The local populace was barely being kept alive by an airlift. Swearing he would never surrender, old Marshal Yan Xishan showed us the vial of cyanide pills that he and his generals vowed to swallow before the Communists captured the city. In the end the Marshal fled, and died peacefully in Taiwan.

Finally, at the climactic million-man Battle of Huai-Hai that sealed Chiang Kai-shek's fate, we stood on a hill with Li Mi, one of his most trusted generals, and watched the epic fight for control of China unfold. Once again, I didn't have to rely on memory to describe the battle scene in the book. My old eyewitness notes, including the following, were vivid enough:

About a hundred soldiers were sprawled over the craggy slope, weapons in their laps, eating their evening bowls of rice. The glowing red sun dropped below the horizon and a white ground mist crawled slowly up the valley floor covering the black line of the Lunghai railroad. Li's adjutant cranked the field phone and shouted curt commands to the forward gun positions. Suddenly the war was on.

Huge muzzle flashes from the 105 mm ballooned from the plain, hung for an instant, and then blinked out. Ahead of the artillery the 37 mm guns of Li's tanks cut red streaks through the blackness. Occasional flares and signal lights lit up the sky. Between the thunderous blasts came the incongruous creak and groan of an oxcart bumping its way across the field below. After an hour the barrage slowed and flames licked the sky. "Now

the infantry," said Li who indicated it was also time for
dinner.

Half a million men died during the Battle of Huai-
Hai, where the Nationalists' eventual defeat opened
the way for the Communist armies to roll south across
the Yangtze River and into the Nationalist capital
of Nanjing, and finally Shanghai. Except for a last-
minute round of executions of suspected Communist
agents carried out by the police in Shanghai, its fall
to the Communists came as a relatively quiet anti-
climax, as my notes below recorded:

> *Seeing Mao's soldiers enter the great metropolis you*
> *couldn't help being impressed by how well armed they*
> *were with Bren guns and Tommy guns. Hand grenades*
> *hung from their belts and bandoliers of cartridges from*
> *their shoulders. But most of them were peasant boys*
> *clearly more amazed at Shanghai than Shanghai was*
> *at them. They gawked at the fancy hotels and movie*
> *palaces. "What day is it?" asked one. "We've been*
> *walking and fighting for a week."*

As I flew out of Shanghai that same May evening
in 1949, I assumed it was for the last time, that I would
never see China again. Peering down at the vanishing
skyline with the Huangpu River snaking through it,

I was gripped by sadness, as if saying goodbye to a rollicking old friend. My old notebook again captured my emotion:

Goodbye, amazing city. It wasn't just your clash between East and West and rich and poor that set you apart. Nor was it your sex and other vices, your everything-for-sale attitude, or your rampant violence and inbred corruption. It was your day-to-day excitement that will never be duplicated.

I was right about that, but wrong about never going back. I have returned many times, several of the visits on assignments for various magazines, continuing on into my late seventies. My interest in China practically became a full-time occupation. Each return visit kept refreshing my memories in a different way.

My first trip back in 1973 was with an Ethiopian delegation led by Emperor Haile Selassie's grand-daughter, Princess Ida. Joining that junket required flying 8,000 miles from Hong Kong to Addis Ababa to pick up a visa, and then doubling back 8,000 miles to Shanghai. It was still very difficult for us American journalists to enter China, and we used any means possible. My notes recorded what had become Shanghai:

The evening ride from the airport was dismal. The city was dark, all the flashy neon replaced by sickly flickering yellow bulbs. The spellbinding cacophony that had kept me awake during my first nights in 1946 had evaporated, having given way to the muffled whirr of thousands of bicycles wheels turning in unison. Shanghai was like a roaring old reprobate who had survived a stroke.

Flying north from Shanghai, there again was the beauty of old China. My reverent mood looking out the window of the plane was unmistakable as I wrote:

Who could ever forget those misty purple peaks marching off to meet the snowy Himalayas, the mighty Yellow and Yangtze rivers slithering like two dusty snakes across the dun-colored Central Plain where my truck convoys had run, and finally the ground turning a pale green as we swooped low over fields of winter cabbage growing right up to the edge of the runway of Beijing's airport.

The main social event during that visit to Beijing was a cocktail reception in the Great Hall of the People hosted by Premier Zhou Enlai, the former brigadier general who in 1947 had dropped in unexpectedly on our UNRRA headquarters in Kaifeng. For two hours, Zhou moved systematically through the assembled throng, shaking hands with all of the visiting Ethiopian dignitaries. After each round of handshakes, a waiter gave the premier a moist washrag to wipe his hands.

Suddenly there he was, the double-barreled boss of China's domestic and foreign policy, extending a hand to me. "Your excellency," I said. "I have some old photographs for your archives." Then I handed him an envelope containing pictures I had taken of the Flooded Area in Henan in 1947. Zhou looked perplexed, but his interpreter accepted the envelope.

My gift to the prime minister was a faux pas of the first order. No breach of protocol was intended, I explained to the deputy foreign minister who was present. I merely hoped that the old photographs might elicit an invitation from the premier to revisit Henan, so that I could retrace the routes of my UNRRA truck convoys.

"That's not possible," replied the deputy foreign minister. "Perhaps some other time."

In 1975 when I returned to Beijing with President Ford I renewed the request in person, and continued sending written requests to the foreign ministry every six months or so. Finally, in 1981 my patience paid off and I was invited to tour the former Flooded Area for an article in *Fortune*. My notes revealed how everything had changed during the intervening thirty-four years:

For two weeks in a Toyota van rented with a driver from the Tourist Auto Car Brigade, and a guide borrowed from the All-China Journalists Association, Helen and I revisited the towns and villages that had been caught in the civil war. Following behind in a jeep were a nurse and medical doctor in case we got sick. Apparently, that was a risk our hosts took seriously, because I was then sixty-one, an age considered quite old in China.

Ribbons of blacktop had replaced the ancient sandy ruts. The formerly barren, silt-covered Central Plain was green with wheat, corn sorghum, soybeans, tobacco, and cotton. The ancient towns to which I had delivered relief supplies still stood. But stripped of their old protective walls, and stretched helter-skelter to accommodate new schools, factories, and workers' apartments, they now encroached on the surrounding farmland.

It was there that we encountered the first signs of China's creeping capitalism, with farmers showing up in local markets to sell some of their produce grown, not on the big communes, but on privately owned plots.

In 1989 *Life* and the CBS *Sunday Morning* show hosted by Charles Kuralt, decided in tandem to send me back to Shanghai yet another time, for the fortieth anniversary of the People's Republic. I was amazed how outspoken the once-docile students had become. Thousands of them were massing every day in the People's Park where the old race course used to be, demanding more opportunity and freedom. But in Shanghai, officials wisely resisted calling in the tanks to fire on the demonstrators, as the authorities in Beijing did ten days later in Tiananmen Square.

After that, I found myself clipping newspaper articles every day about the country's fragile political situation and exploding economy. It was with great anticipation that I returned once again to Shanghai for *Fortune* in 1997 as the British lease on Hong Kong was about to expire. In effect, the two cities were trading places, much of the former Crown Colony's business being transferred to Shanghai. Landing in that seething city I noted:

It was like jumping into a cauldron. The non-stop assault on the senses was caused not only by the impatient honking of thousands of taxis gridlocked on Nanjing Road, or the deafening tattoo of jackhammers biting into bedrock, or the new crop of singsong girls populating hundreds of karaoke bars. It was also caused by the capitalistic fever gripping practically every one of its fourteen million citizens.

Before leaving Shanghai I decided to stop in at the decaying building on the Bund formerly occupied by the Time-Life bureau when I was a young reporter. It currently belonged to the Harbor Navigation

Administration. My interpreter explained to two young clerks poring over a pile of papers up on the third floor that this was where I had written my final dispatches as the Communists marched in. They looked up in disbelief. "This only happens in the movies," one of them exclaimed.

Two years later, when I was seventy-nine years old, *Fortune* sent me back to China for one last time (or so the editor expected it would be) to mark the fiftieth anniversary of the People's Republic. By this time I had already seen how Beijing, Shanghai, and the other coastal cities had been transformed. But what had happened to the four former Nationalist strong-holds—Mukden, Taiyuan, Xuzhou, and Nanjing, where the decisive battles of the civil war had been fought? Were they stuck in a time warp? Or were they also leapfrogging into the twenty-first century? Before ending my long association with China I felt a compelling urge to find out.

Accompanied by my wife and photographer Fritz Hoffmann, I began the return trek in Mukden, renamed Shenyang. The ghost city that was being overrun by Communist General Lin Biao's soldiers in 1948 when I hurriedly left was sprouting glitzy new glass and steel skyscrapers everywhere. High-tech foreign companies had replaced most of the old smokestack-heavy industries. But the Communist economy appeared to be out of kilter. While a good number of the city's 6.8 million people were still unemployed, many others had become affluent and were not averse to being seen in skin-tight Ralph Lauren jeans or wearing flashy Gucci ties. "What a difference half a century makes," I thought.

That was also true in Taiyuan. When I left Marshal Yan Xishan's old walled city, children were begging, not chatting up strangers to practice their English as they were now. The Nationalist arsenal had been converted into a heavy machinery company, while the hills around the city, once honeycombed with Communist gun emplacements, were being mined for coal, iron ore, and gypsum. What caught my eye was a playground with brightly painted swings and slides that had replaced the old dirt airstrip used to keep the city alive during the airlift. Only the massive North Gate, through which Mao's troops finally poured, was preserved as a Communist victory monument.

When I had left Taiyuan the last time, running and ducking to reach the airstrip during a deafening mortar attack, I remember glancing back at the twin pagodas of the Monastery of Eternal Happiness and thinking what a ridiculous name for a place of worship in a war-torn city being put through such torture. When I flew out of Taiyuan on this trip, I gazed down at the shiny twin towers of the new forty-two-story

Shanxi International Trade Center, symbolizing Taiyuan's new capitalist religion.

Returning to Xuzhou, I found the city associated
with the great Battle of Huai-Hai had not become
as modern as Shenyang or Taiyuan. Most of the old
buildings had survived, making it more resonant of the
China I used to know. Yet it was far different than the
panicked city I left in 1949. Nationalist officers were then
rounding up civilians from the refugee-packed streets to
dig trenches and patch the city's protective wall, while
trucks, mule carts, and rickshaws filled with wounded
soldiers straggled in from the battlefield, twenty-five
miles to the east. A military museum had been built
there containing dioramas, three-dimensional maps,
film clips, and photographs showing the Communist
side of the war. "Huai-Hai was like your Gettysburg,"
the museum's curator explained.

What I wanted to do most was to find the nearby
hilltop from which I had observed the fierce Nationalist attack and Communist counter-attack with General
Li Mi. It was the same desire, I think, that has lured
so many American World War II veterans back to the
beaches of Normandy years after the invasion. Etched
in my memory was the sleepless night I spent there,
listening to artillery shells scream overhead, while the
pounding pulse of my oncoming bout of typhoid fever
beat in my ears.

After a series of false starts we finally found the right hill. During the war the little village below had been ringed by mud trenches and pillboxes protecting the big 155 mm Howitzers. Ducks, chickens, pigs, and bare-bottomed children now scampered through the muddy streets. I showed some of the 1949 *Life* photos to a few of the oldsters who had lived through the battle. "That's my grandmother," shouted one, pointing to the picture of an old woman defiantly standing her ground amidst machine-gun positions outside her mud house.

As I climbed the rocky hill to the observation post from which General Li's aide had shouted commands into a field phone directing the Nationalist attack, it was still all so clear in my mind. My reverie was abruptly broken when quarry workers below set off a series of dynamite blasts, a deafening reminder of China's civil war.

If I had gone ahead and accepted Little, Brown's remunerative offer for a China memoir in 1949, it would have lacked the perspective gained during my many subsequent visits. Interest in China has also grown dramatically since then, while I have become a more experienced and better writer, having turned out a number of books on such diverse subjects as war, intuition, world leaders, fishing, even one on all the White House dogs.

The Lyons Press editor's offer for a long-postponed China memoir nevertheless came as a surprise. So many years had passed, and so much had been and was being written about China. But then as the editor reminded me, "Only two or three of you Americans are left who covered the revolution there. You're an endangered species. You better start writing."

My decision to finally go ahead wasn't so much based on the nostalgia that gripped me while reading my old files, but by the idea that I could recapture those old experiences in a fascinating new project— a book—that would probably take at least a year or two to complete. I knew that I needed the challenge, just as so many of my friends do who are writing family memoirs. It's a great way to fill the empty hours that loom ahead for anyone just ending a career. As Napoleon Bonaparte wrote on board the H.M.S. *Bellerophon,* bound for a life of boredom in exile on the island of Elba: "Whatever shall we do in that remote spot? Well, we will write our memoirs." (He escaped before finishing.)

And thinking back to the Little, Brown offer in 1949, would Hollywood have bid then for *Chasing the Dragon,* as I called my memoir? That's doubtful. China was still conceived as a remote and exotic land that spawned mainly Charlie Chan mysteries, not the kind of epic film envisioned now. Today I hold a contract with Universal Pictures for a feature film to be made in collaboration with Tribeca, the New York City company owned in part by Robert DeNiro, who wants to play Henry Luce in the movie. If and when the filming gets started, and is shot in China, I plan to go back one more time, even if I'm a hundred.

{12}

Reliving the Dream

From the preceding chapters it might be assumed that covering China and the rest of the world as a foreign correspondent had consumed so much of my time and energy that I had little passion left for anything else. That's not true. As a former high school pitcher with a pretty fair fastball (but not much else), baseball has always been, and still is, an important part of my life. Today, what I like best is following the rookies as they chase their dreams in the minors before maturing into stars. Maybe for this ninety-year-old fan, it's the vicarious thrill of seeing these young players finally blossom in the Show, as the major leagues are called.

That aspect of the game got the best of me eleven years ago when *Fortune* bought my idea of writing an article on the rapidly expanding business of minor league baseball. Behind that boom, I quickly discovered, was not just a swelling crop of eager young players, but a number of retired men, who being more than mere fans, were finally fulfilling their boyhood dreams of playing for the Yankees, Dodgers, or some other major-league team by belatedly becoming minor-league owners. Of course, to invest in baseball in their "golden years," they needed to have some spare gold. But what a wonderful way to spend it. The important thing was they were doing what they loved, and at the same time gaining satisfaction by doing something that benefits the community.

You've probably never heard of most of their teams. They bear strange names like Lugnuts, Lumberjacks, Quakes, River Dogs, and Rock Cats. Yet they are among more than 230 minor league clubs now playing their hearts out in shiny new stadiums (seating on average seven thousand fans) with cheap seats ($2 to $10) from coast to coast. Thanks to these retired businessmen/owners, a family of four can watch a pretty good brand of baseball, with a round of hotdogs and sodas thrown in, for less than thirty bucks.

The proliferating minor-league teams and their loyal rooters remind me of a piece of advice from the writer Jacques Barzun. "Whoever wants to know the heart and mind of America," he wrote in *God's Country and Mine*, "had better learn baseball, the rules and realities of the game—and do it by watching first some high school or small-town teams."

I had never written about baseball before and felt like the old dog trying to learn new tricks. But then neither had the new crop of owners used their sophisticated marketing skills on a sport before—former corporate leaders like Floyd Hall, the retired chairman of Kmart and owner of New Jersey Jackals, and Dan Burke, the former CEO of Cap Cities/ABC, owner of the Portland, Maine, Sea Dogs. If Burke can't be there in the ballpark to watch his Sea Dogs play every night, he insists on having the game's statistics e-mailed to him at home before going to bed. "I don't sleep well if I don't know how the team did," he says.

But it isn't just the former business leaders who are fulfilling their youthful baseball dreams that way. Most of the ticket takers, concession operators, and ushers working at minor-league stadiums are retired men (and a few retired women) who'd rather spend their summer afternoons or evenings at a ballgame, earning a little extra grocery money, than staying at home. And a good number of the fans themselves are geezers living on limited fixed incomes who can still afford a bleacher seat, and one with a better view of the action than is provided by most big league box seats. Perhaps that's why baseball is called the National *Pastime*: "Something that amuses and serves to make the time pass agreeably," according to Webster.

To get started on my *Fortune* article, I picked the

New Britain, Connecticut, Rock Cats, a Minnesota Twins farm team in the Double-A Eastern League, within easy driving distance from my home. Standing in front of the modern red brick and steel stadium when I arrived was Bill Dowling, president, general manager, and principal owner. Impeccably dressed in a blue blazer, striped tie, and tan pants he was surveying the cars streaming into the blacktop parking lot. "Looks like a sell-out," he said optimistically. Then as if he were the host of a private party being given at his home, he continued greeting many of the arriving ticket-holders with a jovial handshake or friendly slap on the back. "It's like being a congressman," he said. "These are my constituents and I've got to listen to what they have to say, and let them know I appreciate their support."

Pleased with the prospect of a sell-out crowd, Bill headed back inside the stadium where he roamed the cavernous concourse under the stands, checking on everything from ticket sales to the cleanliness of the toilets. Not exactly the duties you'd expect of a successful trial lawyer who still spends one day a week in New York City defending clients. "The food business is leased out to a catering company," he explained, "so I don't have to check on that. But it still produces a healthy chunk of revenue and helps to keep our tickets moderately priced from $3.50 to $10."

Bill, I discovered, got his start in baseball as a Little League pitcher in Holyoke, Massachusetts. Big for his age, he mowed down the smaller batters like a farmer reaping wheat in a field. In his last year he won twenty-seven games. Later as a baseball-loving lawyer, he had the advantage of serving as vice president and general counsel of the New York Yankees. But as a neophyte owner in New Britain, he quickly recognized that to make money out of a minor-league franchise he also had to attract non-baseball fanatics by offering what he called "a wholesome afternoon or night out with the wife and kids."

Besides baseball, that meant providing reasonably priced sodas, beer, hotdogs, and souvenirs, as well as non-stop, non-baseball entertainment. "You have to be innovative," he said. Before the game he let local Little League kids swarm out on the field to take a bow, while the players canvassed the crowd signing autographs. He filled the dead time between innings with clumsy clowns racing tiny tots around the bases (the clown always lost), "dizzy bat races," tug-of-wars, three-legged races, and for those who didn't leave after the seventh-inning stretch to put the kids to bed, he provided fireworks for the final treat. It struck me that the whole performance on the field in New Britain, as it was in many other minor league parks, had been inspired more by Walt Disney than Abner Doubleday.

Even so, baseball was still the main attraction. And today the minor-league players often put on a more exciting show than their big-league brothers. Hoping to catch the eye of a scout (usually a retirement job for old players), these aspiring youngsters risk bodily injury to make spectacular plays that the multimillion-dollar big league players won't chance. As a result, strong-armed young hurlers light up the pitch-speed gauge with fastballs well into the 90-miles-per-hour range, while their acrobatic teammates make diving catches and headlong slides, unafraid of tearing a ligament or fracturing a shoulder.

Bill Dowling, I could see, loves his involvement in the whole operation. And that's what's important about any post-retirement job. He enjoys his association with the rising young stars, even though they are the property of the Minnesota Twins, and can be taken away from him and promoted to Triple-A Rochester at any crucial moment during the Eastern League pennant race. He rarely misses a home game and never sits, but stands in the aisle behind the batters' on-deck circle to watch the play. "This is my elixir," he claims. "I feel that it's adding exciting years to my life."

Bill insisted that I, as the visiting representative of a national magazine, should be given the chance to throw out the ceremonial first ball, fulfilling one of my own boyhood dreams of pitching off a professional mound. This was an honor usually reserved for a local business leader, a way of helping to promote his company.

As I walked across the infield to the mound, the thick groves of pines and maples growing up to the outfield fence cast cool shadows on the field. Suddenly the lights snapped on there I was in the center of the glare with seven thousand fans and fourteen thousand eyes peering down at me.

"Will my old high school fastball still have some zip after sixty-five years?" I wondered. "Will it pop into the catcher's mitt with a loud crack as it once did? What number will flash on the illuminated pitch-speed gauge mounted on the right field fence?" The two starting pitchers had both reached numbers in the low nineties during their warm-ups. "I'll be happy to register a sixty," I thought. But as I began my painstakingly slow wind-up, dragging out this once-in-a-lifetime experience as long as possible, the catcher crouched behind home plate suddenly looked half a mile away. It was like I was seeing him through the wrong end of a telescope.

I finally brought my arm down, putting all the power I could muster behind the pitch. To my horror I watched the ball arc slowly through the air and drop like a stone in the dirt in front of home plate. The crowd let out a sympathetic groan as catcher A.

J. Pierzynski, who would soon star for the Twins and then for the Chicago White Sox, scooped it out of the dirt and then tossed it back to me for a keepsake.

By the time I completed the article, I had thrown out a dozen other ceremonial first balls as a photographer and had crisscrossed the country from Rancho Cucamonga, California, to Lansing, Michigan, to Houston, Texas, to Trenton, New Jersey. Everywhere we found that the owners, like Bill Dowling, had added various amenities to their ballparks including: swimming pools, hot tubs, rock climbing walls, playgrounds, and picnic pavilions. On hot days in Charleston, South Carolina, we discovered belatedly that the owners of the River Dogs had warned their fans to come wearing bathing suits because they were likely to be doused with fire hoses. We were, and had to sit through the game in sopping wet clothes.

Covering all those young teams was so refreshing for an old reporter that I tried to think of some way I could spend an entire summer going to minor league baseball games. Eventually, in 2005 when I was eighty-five, I hit upon the idea of picking two aspiring young pitchers, one a Latino, the other an American, but both chasing the same dream of playing in the majors. Hopefully, by the end of the season one of them might make it to the majors, and I would have enough material for a book. It was a risky venture. But then as Woody Allen says, "If you're not failing now and then, it's a sign that you're not doing anything very innovative." But in this case, if I failed I would still have had a good time. Bill Dowling and the Rock Cats, I knew, would provide the kind of close cooperation required.

Starting at spring training in Fort Myers, Florida, Helen and I sat in one of the coach's towers watching three games going on at one time. Baseballs were flying in every direction like flocks of wild birds. As an artist with little knowledge of the game, she enjoyed sketching the action. Finally with the advice of Jim Rantz, in charge of player development for the Twins, I picked my two pitchers for the book: Francisco Liriano, twenty-one, a six-foot-two left-hander originally plucked from the sandlots of the Dominican Republic, and right-hander Justin Olson, twenty-five, a former Big Ten star at the University of Illinois. Both were known for the bullets they threw, though Liriano had the edge in that department hitting ninety-six and ninety-seven mph on the pitch-speed gauge, and reminding fans of his idol, the Twins Venezuelan ace, Johan Santana.

As the season progressed, Helen and I enjoyed the dramatically changing scenery that she was able to sketch as we drove our old Ford Explorer between Portland, Maine, and Bowie, Maryland, to cover the two pitchers. Liriano had the advantage of being part of the Rock Cats' starting rotation, while Olson, an occasional starter, spent most of his time in the bullpen as a "middle-innings reliever." But then Olson was called upon to pitch more frequently, so I considered the competition between them about even.

In mid-June, without any advance warning, Liriano was called up by the Rochester Red Wings, in the Triple-A International League, the last rung on the ladder to Minnesota and the big leagues. This was a great break for the young Dominican. But it expanded the territory my wife and I had to cover from Quebec, Ontario, to Durham, North Carolina, where the local team had provided the inspiration for the 1988 hit movie *Bull Durham* (one of several films, including *The Naturalist* and *Field of Dreams*, that helped to trigger the resurging interest in minor-league baseball).

Liriano got off to an amazing start with the Red Wings. We watched him mow down one batter after another in Rochester, Syracuse, and Pawtucket, Rhode Island, by alternating his blazing fastball with a devastating slider. The sports writers nicknamed him the "Zero Hero" because of all of the consecutive scoreless innings he pitched.

A daily diet of baseball was a little hard to digest. So on our travels we took several picturesque detours, stopping for lunch one day at Fort Byron, a quaint town on an offshoot of the Erie Canal, and spending a night with friends at their summer home on Lake Canandaigua, surrounded by spectacular waterfront gardens. In Watkins Glen, at the foot of Seneca Lake, we had a picnic in front of Montour Falls, or She-Qua-Ga (Tumbling Falls), as a historic marker indicated the Indians called it. The sign also revealed that in about 1820 Louis Philippe, who later became King of France, made a sketch of the falls that is now in the Louvre. Helen also sketched the falls, and we decided we'd have to compare the two sketches the next time we were in Paris. A drought, however, had reduced the Tumbling Falls that Helen sketched to a wispy flow, barely wetting the sheer rock wall behind it.

By early August it was time for us to catch up again with Olson and the Rock Cats. We planned a leisurely drive through the Berkshires, with a possible night off at Tanglewood to take in a concert. We finally arrived in New Britain in time for the last two games of a three-game series against Trenton, a Yankee farm team loaded with powerful young sluggers. Olson, we discovered, had been picked to pitch the last game of the series on Sunday afternoon.

Justin never was able to disguise his boyish enthusiasm, so I could tell right away that he was pretty excited about taking the mound against the number-two team in the league. It also turned out that his wife Jamie, his mother Dawn, and his grandparents were all flying in from Chicago to watch him pitch. So besides having a family reunion, he wanted to show them how well his career was progressing.

I watched him out on the sun-drenched mound throwing warm-up pitches with easy rhythmical motions, belying much effort, even though the pitch-speed gauge registered ninety-two and ninety-three mph. Maybe it was because his relatives were sitting directly behind me waiting for the game to begin that I, myself, felt the enormous weight of being out there on the mound in that situation. Yet, Justin looked cool and relaxed popping one pitch after another into the mitt of catcher Gabby Torres. "He's one cool Rock Cat," I thought.

Without warning the game began and the balls and strikes were being counted. Olson got two strikes on the leadoff batter. He worked the count up to 3 and 2 before nicking the inside corner of the plate for a called third strike. He also struck out the second batter. I was sitting next to Chicago Cubs' scout Lukas McKnight, who'd come to take a look at Olson as a future prospect they might want to buy. "He looks pretty sharp to me," I said, but Lukas didn't respond.

Next it was Melky Cabrera's turn to bat. Melky, who would soon be patrolling the outfield for the Yankees, swung on the first pitch and muscled a single over the shortstop's head. That brought up the brawny clean-up hitter Shelley Duncan, who led the Eastern League with twenty-seven home runs. But that didn't faze Olson even though the gopher ball was his nemesis.

Duncan swung and missed, twisting his body off balance, as the pitch-speed gauge registered another ninety-four. Olson fired a second fastball. Duncan swung and missed again, this time lunging for a low-and-away ball, way out of the strike zone. With the count 2 and 0, Justin grooved a fastball, this one right down the middle. Shelley swung, and as the next morning's *New Britain Herald* reported: "The ball may have reached all the way to the High School on the first bounce."

"After two strikes, he should have thrown a curve-ball," Lukas the scout said. "A curveball would have gotten him back in rhythm."

I couldn't help feel Justin's disappointment. He'd been so looking forward to proving to his family that professional baseball is worth pursuing, even if the pay in the minors is poor. But he had no time to commiser-ate. The next batter, Eric Duncan (not related to Shel-ley), was also a formidable hitter, and as Lukas pointed out, was the number one prospect in the entire Yankee organization.

Olson still had his searing speed—and his confi-dence as well, it appeared. He blew two fastballs right past Eric Duncan for strikes. Then as if Olson had heard Lukas's comment about the need to regain his rhythm, he threw two looping curveballs that missed, sending the count to 2 and 2. Olson's speed was so impressive I felt sure he would retire the side with another fastball. My prediction proved to be 50 percent correct. Olson fired another bullet. Eric Duncan swung hard, and like his namesake, sent the ball flying over the left field fence—the fifteenth home run Olson had given up in less than one hundred innings.

It didn't really matter what happened after that. Olson struck out Mike Coleman, the last batter, and two more hitters before being replaced after the fourth inning with the score still 3 to 0. Trenton went on to win 4 to 2. Lukas charitably commented that Olson did better than the scoreboard indicated. "Most of his pitches were pretty crisp," he said, repeating the word he favored for quickly released bullets.

But manager Stan Cliburn, miffed about Olson's poor choice of pitches, told reporters afterwards, "We lost the game in the first inning." It was the first time I ever heard the manager pin the blame for a defeat on one player.

I knew then and there that those two bad pitches had cost Olson the chance of ever pitching in the major leagues, and I knew precisely how he felt, reliving my own crush of disappointment when Dartmouth's baseball coach, Jeff Tesreau, a former spitball special-ist with the New York Giants, watched me throw, and quickly indicated that I didn't have what it takes to make the team.

Helen and I had come to the New Britain ball-park with our bags packed for the first leg of the drive back to Rochester to catch up again with Liriano. For-tunately for us, and I guess for Olson too, the game ended early. That suited us fine because we hoped to see at least the last innings of the night game in Oneonta, where the farm team of the Detroit Tigers was celebrating the hundredth anniversary of the local stadium. I had seen a few games in that antique ballpark in 1991 when I was a trustee at Hartwick Col-lege. Oneonta was then a Yankee farm club, starring pitcher Andy Pettitte and catcher Jorge Posada.

The game there wasn't scheduled to start until 7 p.m., plenty of time to make the trip without speed-ing or resorting to thruways. We stuck to old Route 23 that winds through a series of beautiful old towns in the southwest corner of Massachusetts—Monterey, Great Barrington, and Egremont—then crosses into New York State and over the Rip Van Winkle Bridge. Glancing back at the river we could see perched high on the eastern bank the ornate Persian-style castle called Olana, which was the last home of the celebrated nine-teenth century landscape painter Frederic Church.

Ahead the road plunged deep into the Catskills Mountains and on to Oneonta. All the way I kept thinking about Olson and his family. What did they think, watching those two momentous home runs sail over the fence? They had been so excited the night before, anticipating a triumphant day on the mound for Justin. Then Boom! Boom! The game was over before it had really begun. How many careers in any profession ever end that precipitously?

The game in Oneonta had already begun by the time we arrived. Dick Miller, then the president of Hartwick College, introduced Helen and me to the home team's two venerable owners, Sam Nader, the city's eighty-six-year-old former mayor, and ninety-two-year-old Sid Levine. Both men had spent their entire long lives involved in professional baseball. Dick had endeared himself to them by providing rooms for their players, and for the visiting team members as well, in the college dorms that were empty during the summer.

Sitting there listening to Sam as the Oneonta Tigers battled the Jamestown, New York Jammers, I felt we were back in the old bush-league era of my youth. The ancient cement grandstand, silhouetted by the lights, stood like a hundred-year-old ghost behind us. Just a sprinkling of fans remained sitting on its hard seats, most of them having slipped down to the more comfortable field boxes enclosed by blue iron railings, which Sam claimed were hand-me-downs from the Syracuse SkyChiefs. "They built a new stadium up there in 1996 and shipped us their old box seats," he said. "The batting cage is a hand-me-down too," he added. "It was a gift from the Yankees in 1961."

Coming into the ballpark I noticed the tickets cost $5 for adults and $4 for children. "In the early days," Sam said, "fans had the choice of paying or watching the game for free from atop the Delaware & Hudson freight cars parked next door. Today, sixteen of the thirty-eight home games are sponsored by local businesses. On those nights nobody has to pay."

I was surprised that the Oneonta team was a Detroit farm club, although I knew the Yankees had moved its Single-A franchise in the New York–Pennsylvania League into fancy new digs on Staten Island. "It doesn't matter where the players come from or what the team's called," Sam said handing me a copy of the ballpark's special hundredth-anniversary program. "When you read this you'll see that our team has had many different names, starting with the Oneonta Red Lions."

As the Tigers scored a run and eked out a victory in the ninth inning and both owners stood up to cheer, I couldn't help but notice how spry they seemed, even though they, like their stadium, were relics of a bygone baseball era. "We've owned the franchise for forty-one years" announced Sam proudly. "And we hardly ever miss a home game." The two old codgers reminded me of what Bill Dowling said about baseball being the elixir that is adding exciting years to his life.

It was an exciting summer for Helen and me. While completing the baseball circuit we also enjoyed several interesting cultural experiences, including visits to the New Britain Museum of American Art with its fine collection of Hudson River School paintings; the Corning Glass Museum in Corning, New York, with its incredible exhibit of 3,500 years of glassmaking; a night at the Glimmer Glass Opera, named after what James Fenimore Cooper called the mirror-smooth Otsego Lake in Cooperstown; and the George Eastman International Museum of Photography and Film in Rochester.

By the end of the summer Helen had compiled a scrapbook full of lively sketches and I ended up with several notebooks crammed full of information about minor-league baseball and the diverging careers of Justin Olson and Francisco Liriano—enough for a book titled *Throwing Bullets: A Tale of Two Pitchers Chasing the Dream.*

Liriano was called up by Minnesota in September of that same year, achieving his dream of pitching in the majors. Today, he is an ace member of the Twins starting rotation. Olson was released by the Twins organization and spent the next season pitching for the Fargo-Moorhead Red Hawks, an unaffiliated team in the independent Northern League, before I lost track of him. But with a college degree in kinesiology, he fortunately had another profession to fall back on.

The Rock Cats have been so successful, attracting more fans each season, that Bill Dowling, now sixty-eight, is looking for a second franchise to buy. Sam Nader and Sid Levine, now ninety-one and ninety-seven respectively, sadly had their Tigers franchise bought out from under them in 2010 when it was moved to Norwich, Connecticut. "I sure wasn't happy about that," said Sam, still athletic enough to keep his golf score lower than his age.

Oneonta's long history of baseball will continue, but with a team made up of college stars, appropriately named the Outlaws according to Sam, who refuses to have anything to do with them. The sad end to his and Sid's long association with Oneonta's teams reminded me of the cautionary words spoken by a retired high school principal working as head usher for the Portland Sea Dogs: "Behind the boom in minor-league baseball," he warned, "are also many broken dreams—players who won't ever make it to the big leagues, and owners who thought there was a pot of gold at the end of the rainbow in center field."

Sid and Sam were never in it for the money. Their reward came from the satisfaction of bringing professional baseball to a city of only fifteen thousand residents. And like my own interest in the minors, they got great pleasure from seeing a few of their former young players, especially Andy Petitte and Jorge Posada, become Major League stars.

{13}

Finally, a Feeling of Closure

For several mornings after my eightieth birthday I was awakened by the same harrowing dream. It started with the strains of "White Christmas"—the signal used at dawn some twenty-five years earlier to evacuate Saigon. "This is it," the U.S. Armed Forces Radio confirmed. "Everybody out!"

In the dream all of us correspondents and photographers poured out of the Continental Palace Hotel into the empty square in front of the old French opera house to board buses for Tan Son Nhut Air Base. Pillars of black smoke were rising from the hangars, under artillery fire. Seconds later, a tremendous explosion rocked the terminal building where we were supposed to wait.

The dream would start to fizzle before I could board one of the big Marine Sea Stallion helicopters for the flight to safety to one of the U.S. Navy ships cruising off the coast. There I was, the last American left in Saigon with no way to escape. Then I woke up.

This recurring dream got me wondering whether I should consider going back to write a twenty-fifth anniversary article on the fall of Saigon. I still retained many disturbing images even though I'd already visited the city once since the war. The American evacuation on April 30, 1975, had come so suddenly it was as if the curtain had come down in the middle of a play. I still needed to know how the story ended. As William Faulkner wrote about a writer's responsibility to his art: "He has a dream. It anguishes him so much he must get rid of it. He has no peace until then."

But was I spry enough at eighty to undergo the rigors of the firsthand reporting required, like climbing through the labyrinthine Cu Chi Tunnels burrowed under Saigon by the Viet Cong to smuggle insurgents into the city? And it would take a lot of hard digging to find a few of the old enemy leaders, even though I had covered Vietnam on and off since 1948 when French Foreign Legionnaires, backed by black troops from Mozambique, were fighting Ho Chi Minh's Communist rebels.

In those early days I had gone on such foolhardy missions as accompanying French mercenary pilots, flying lumbering old German World War II tri-motor Junkers to parachute food and ammunition to Dien

Bien Phu and the other isolated hilltop fortresses. I still recalled my concern—no alarm—at watching those pilots consume their pre-flight breakfasts consisting of a croissant washed down with a couple of swigs of cognac. It never occurred to me then that the U.S. would eventually get sucked into what would evolve from France's colonial war. But as the prolific American author Louis L'Amour wrote: "There will come a time when you think everything is finished. That will be the beginning."

Truman and Eisenhower sensibly refused to let that happen, and Kennedy took only a tentative step in that direction by sending in military advisors starting in 1962. It may be an apocryphal story, but back about 1940, when soldiers from China (Vietnam's longtime foe) were pouring south through the border town of Dong Dang, Franklin Roosevelt is alleged to have spurned a French request for American troops, with the comment, "We will not go to war for any Ding Dong."

As *Time*'s Saigon bureau chief for the last two years of the war, witnessing curbside assassinations in the city and so many other cruel and unnecessary killings out in the countryside, I often thought of Vietnam as our senseless Ding Dong war. Not Lyndon Johnson's war, although the furor at home caused by his escalation of it and the resulting loss of some 58,000

American lives had forced him to forgo running for a second four-year term.

Returning twenty-five years later, haunted by so many old memories, I knew would not be easy. It never is. Any traumatic experience, whether it be a whipping given by an irate father or the loss of a loved one, is painful to look back on. Returning I knew would open old scars, and raise the anger in me once again. And if I found some of our former enemies, would they talk to me? Especially the Viet Cong general who engineered the brazen Lunar New Year attack on the U.S. embassy in 1968. Remarkably, nine VC commandos had shot their way inside the grounds guarded by U.S. Marines and Army MPs. All of the attackers were killed, as were five of the American guards. But television footage of that stunning blow—more than any other event in the war—made Americans back home question trying to defeat an enemy that was often invisible until he opened fire.

And what about Americans who had fought there, and come back to launch businesses with their former enemies? Would they tell me their war stories? Or would they fear Communist government reprisals if they described some of the military actions in which they had taken part? The tremendous effort required to get a good story seemed daunting. Yet the Vietnam War was, in my opinion, the greatest blight on my generation of Americans. Writing an anniversary article might finally give me a feeling of closure. As Longfellow wrote: "Great is the art of beginning, but greater the art is of ending."

The decision was made easier when *Fortune* asked if I would go back with photographer David Burnett and describe the changes that had taken place during the past twenty-five years in what was now officially called Ho Chi Minh City. "Spend a month there," the editor said. "See if you can't catch the contradictions of a city caught between a Communist and capitalist economy."

I knew only one American left from the war days, a lawyer with the unusual name Sesto Vecchi. He had set up an office in Saigon during the war and kept it open after the American withdrawal. It was through him that on my first day back I found myself on a chartered motor launch, cruising the same waters used by the thousands of boat people packed dangerously into anything that would float to flee Saigon twenty-five years ago. Only on this boat five American executives, all formally attired in starched shirts and silk ties, implausibly puffing Havana cheroots and sipping wine, were reciting stanzas from Robert Service's Yukon ballad, "The Cremation of Sam McGee." Once again I wondered if I was dreaming. Sesto Vecchi, chief muse and founder of this little literary group of expatriates called the Cigar & Poetry Society, assured me that I was not.

"We do this periodically to keep from getting too stressed out," explained Chris Tragakis, the local manager of American International Assurance. A former rifle platoon leader with the 35th Infantry Division, he was wounded at Pleiku in 1966. By 2000 he was starting his second post-war stint in Saigon, recruiting agents to peddle insurance policies for AIA. "My wife's a real trouper," he said. "But she thinks we're crazy coming back here to live."

Maybe not so crazy. Saigon, I found, was a city of excitement and promise. And by almost any measure a much more prosperous place than it was during the war. Then I had reported how American soldiers, sailors, and Marines had pumped hundreds of millions of dollars into the economy. Most of it went for booze, drugs, and prostitutes. All of those things were still available, but less openly and far less abundantly. Now most of the foreign money was building new roads, high-tech factories, and glitzy hotels with skybars and rooftop swimming pools. Not surprisingly, though, the growth rate was being stymied by the Communist bureaucracy. "The trouble," Sesto explained, "is the old revolutionary leaders in Hanoi, who spent years fighting capitalism, are in control."

Still, I found the magnetic pull of this slightly seedy "Paris of the Orient" was its vibrant energy and unabashed entrepreneurial spirit. "Never mind the peeling paint and cracked facades of the old French residences," I jotted in my notebook. "The shops bulge with watches, TVs, VCRs, and karaoke players, and everybody seems to be in perpetual motion." I was glad to be back in the new Saigon.

Strolling along the sidewalks, however, was just as hazardous as ever. Legless beggars, shoeshine boys, mothers lugging sleeping babies, and tiny barefoot flower girls plucked at the skirts and trouser legs—and heart strings—of passing tourists, selling everything from postcards and chewing gum to copies of *The Quiet American*, Graham Greene's novel about Saigon in the 1950s. "Why not?" they wailed when you spurned one of their offerings. "How about this?" they asked, hopefully proffering another item, while showing off their rudimentary English.

A number of famous landmarks remained. The old Continental Hotel (though it had dropped *Palace* from its name) looked pretty much the same as when our *Time* magazine bureau occupied a second-floor suite. But the elevated outdoor cafe known as the Continental Shelf, where we correspondents collected rumors and traded war stories, had been glassed in and converted to the Ristorante Venezia. The hotel's brand new bar featured a B-52 cocktail (Bailey's Irish Cream, Kahlua, and Grand Marnier, set aflame), an ironic name for this lethal concoction, considering the damage done to Vietnam by American bombers.

Unchanged, however, was the ornate old Rex Hotel where JUSPAO (Joint U.S. Public Affairs Office) spokesmen gave their afternoon war briefings, including the daily VC body count, dubbed the Five O' Clock Follies. But I noted that in this commercial hub where a third of the population wasn't yet born in 1975, VC stood for venture capitalist, not Viet Cong.

The Presidential Palace that Ho Chi Minh's tanks smashed their way into the day after we left Saigon had been renamed the Reunification Palace. It looked the same, but had been turned into a museum. I found it eerie visiting the office where I had interviewed President Nguyen Van Thieu shortly before he fled. The rumor had spread that he'd already shipped a planeload of gold to Paris to take care of his retirement. As I once again stood behind Thieu's clean desk, his pledge, "I will not resign," resonated in my head.

One of my main endeavors, on that return trip to Saigon, was to try to locate General Tran Bach Dang, organizer of the devastating Lunar New Year attack on the American embassy. After many false starts I finally found him, frail but a still peppery seventy-four, living in a beautifully landscaped Saigon villa.

"This place used to belong to your diplomats," he said through a translator. "I lived next door and observed all their comings and goings." He then described how he had smuggled ten thousand civilian-clad troops into Saigon, mainly through the Cu Chi Tunnels, for simultaneous attacks, not only on our embassy, but on numerous other key installations as well.

"Do you still bear animosity toward Americans?" I asked him. "We have a saying," said the former Viet Cong commander, "If your enemy falls off his horse, you stop fighting."

After being away from Saigon for so long I was also excited to locate a Vietnamese businessman whom I had known during the war, Nguyen Xuan Oanh, or Jack Owen, as we Americans used to call this Harvard-trained economist. At eighty, he was still working as a consultant, with an impressive list of international clients, including R.R. Donnelly, Conoco, and Mobil. He complained that Doi Moi, the Communist government policy of economic renewal, was being implemented much too slowly. "There's a joke circulating in Saigon," he told me. "What has the Vietnamese government succeeded in doing that the U.S. couldn't?" Answer: "Defeat the Vietnamese people."

Corruption, which severely hampered the American economic aid program during the war, I discovered, was again rampant. A new Enterprise Law had been passed, eliminating the need for certain business licenses. However, the various licensing authorities still insisted on being paid under the table. And a year earlier, the customs office in Saigon had been closed for three weeks, because all of the officials who could sign papers were temporarily in jail.

My most nostalgic moment during the return visit came at an emotional reunion with Pham Xuan An, the only Vietnamese reporter to have worked for *Time*. I still considered him a good friend, although as his former boss I had suspected for some time that his loyalties were divided between the magazine and his country. I had no way to prove this, but it weighed on my conscience. I worried that as a possible spy for the Viet Cong, he could endanger our lives.

In the years after the U.S. military evacuation, the Vietnamese press treated An as a hero, a pretty good indication that he'd been passing information gathered by *Time*'s correspondents to the Viet Cong. To his credit, though, I don't believe he ever intentionally fed me misinformation, or misled our correspondents on the progress of the war.

We met at Givral's, a combination coffee shop, bar, and rumor mill across the street from the Continental Hotel. Gaunt, gravel-voiced, and intense as ever at seventy-two, he seemed the same old An, full of information about local politics and the state of the economy.

I reminded him that on the fateful day in 1975 when the U.S. evacuated Saigon, and we walked together out of the Continental Hotel and said good-bye, his last words to me were, "Don't worry. You'll be all right."

"Did you know then," I asked him, "that the North Vietnamese army wouldn't enter Saigon until the next day?" An didn't respond. Only much later did I realize the answer was clear. He knew.

When An died in 2006 I was surprised to learn that he was buried with the full military honors of a Viet Cong brigadier general. Perhaps I'm naïve, but I still believe he had trod a careful line not to deceive us.

That's more than I can say about Lyndon Johnson, who campaigned for reelection in 1964 with the promise of not sending more American troops to Vietnam. I was then the assistant managing editor of *Life* in charge of the magazine's news coverage. The war was still sputtering along pretty much as it was when Kennedy created the U.S. Military Assistance Command, Vietnam—or MACV as it was known. However, the number of U.S. troops assigned to MACV had been creeping up slowly from the initial cadre of 3,200 to 22,000 by election day. Throughout the campaign Johnson had repeatedly pledged not to send over any more American boys. "The U.S. must neither retreat nor expand the war," he declared.

As one of Henry Luce's key editors at that time, I was expected to lasso a governor, senator, or cabinet member from time to time to have dinner with the boss. Soon after the election that the Johnson-Humphrey ticket won by a landslide, it occurred to me that the vice president-elect would give Luce a good conversational workout. Talking, I knew from a couple of dusk-to-dawn sessions with Humphrey at a mutual friend's home in Washington, was what he liked to do most. However, I worried that he might not let the editor-in-chief get a word in.

Dinner in the Time Inc. boardroom was set for 7 p.m. One of the *Life* correspondents in Washington had agreed to escort Humphrey up from the capital. I had also invited a couple of writers from my "newsfront" department to join us. By 8 p.m. Humphrey hadn't arrived. Luce had downed a stiff bourbon and was showing his impatience, while the rest of us, having polished off a straight-up martini or two, were trying to keep the conversation rolling without our guest of honor.

At 8:30, still no sign of the vice president-elect, but plenty of signs of the editor-in-chief's agitation. He was never one to suffer delays easily. One of the best-known Luce stories circulating the Time & Life Building involved a flight of his to Europe in which the plane, after sitting on the runway for an hour, was brought back to the gate for repairs. Exasperated, Luce called his secretary and told her to get on the horn to his old friend Juan Trippe, Pan American's president, to say that was no way to run an airline. Ten minutes later she called back. "Mr. Luce," she said, "Mr. Trippe says you're on TWA."

Of course, there were jokes, too, about the "Happy Warrior," as Humphrey was known, having a blind spot where most people have a clock. His unquenchable loquaciousness had kept him running late from one end of the campaign to the other. But his delay now had gone beyond the humorous stage.

"Is this man always so atrociously behind schedule?" asked Luce, who I suspected was further rankled by the way our missing guest had helped bury his friend and Arizona neighbor, Barry Goldwater, at the polls in November. No Republican candidate for president had been given a worse trouncing.

"Let's start without him," snapped Luce. But the minute we sat down at the long oval table, in strode Humphrey spewing apologies a mile a minute. The dinner was a bust. Luce let Humphrey do all the talking, and as soon as the meal was finished, said good night and left.

Luce's hasty departure left a couple of my writers and me with the vice president-elect to entertain for the rest of the evening. We grabbed an unopened bottle of scotch from the bar and accompanied our guest to his suite in the Hilton. For the next four hours we sipped scotch and grilled him on what Lyndon Johnson planned to do about Vietnam.

Was the president really determined to hold U.S. troop strength to the 22,000 MACV advisors? Or was his campaign promise so much political palaver? Humphrey swore Johnson meant what he said.

I reminded the man about to become vice president that when Johnson had his job, Kennedy sent him on a fact-finding mission to Vietnam. "Remember how Johnson drove his translators crazy with his folksy Texas hill-country talk?" I asked Humphrey. "'The Communist fox is loose,' he told South Vietnam's president. 'He's after the chickens. And you live in the chicken coop!'" Humphrey smiled. He remembered all right.

But on that trip as vice president, Johnson hadn't minced words about whipping the Viet Cong. "We're going to nail the coonskin to the wall," he promised the press corps in Saigon.

"Are you sure," I asked Humphrey, "that Johnson isn't still trying to nail that coonskin to the wall? And remember back then he also predicted, 'If we throw in the towel in Vietnam, the vast Pacific becomes a Red Sea.'"

"Forget all that stuff about coonskins and a red Pacific," replied Humphrey. "The president has a chastened view of Vietnam."

The memory of that long, not entirely sober night with Humphrey kept coming back to me as our troop buildup had swelled to 500,000 and the annual bill for the war ballooned to $33 billion. Either Johnson had changed his mind, I decided, or he had lied to the voters in 1964—and to his vice president-elect.

Unlike our Vietnamese reporter, Pham Xuan An, whose hidden role was celebrated upon his death, in Lyndon Johnson's case, whether or not he planned secretly all along to raise the stakes in the war, we will never know. For me, however, I felt that I had left Saigon in the year 2000, for the last time. There was no need to go back again. I had seen the last act of the play, and it had ended much better than I thought it would.

{14}

Cruising into the Nineties

During my wife Helen's childbearing years obstetricians couldn't accurately predict the sex of a baby. So it was that we had four sons named Cynthia—who soon after their arrival became Dana, Douglas, Nicholas, and Marcus, in that order. Since then our family has expanded to include Janice, a daughter-in-law; William, a grandson; and Emilie, a "significant other." Today, they could hardly be more widely dispersed around the country, living in Dallas; Port Hueneme, California; Boston; and New York City.

To celebrate my ninetieth birthday I decided to try to bring everybody together on some kind of an expedition. Not an easy chore. For Helen's and my fiftieth wedding anniversary in 2002, our son Marc had surprised us by borrowing a 110-foot yacht with a crew of five, including a Cordon Bleu chef, from a wealthy friend for a week-long voyage in the Bahamas. There was no way I could match that.

Still, I wanted to do something special that would entice everybody to join in. On reaching this big Nine-O milestone, family had become the most important thing in my life. But a family has highly diverse interests, so the bait had to be pretty appealing to hook them all. I considered renting a house in Tuscany. Friends of ours who spend their summers on Block Island, as we do, had one available in mid-June. But that would have involved cooking and housekeeping. I wanted our family get-together to be work-free.

Then an attractive possibility materialized almost by itself. Every couple of years the Time-Life Alumni Society, consisting of retired writers, editors, and advertising sales representatives, organizes some kind of a trip for its members. For its 2010 excursion TLAS was offering a one-week roundtrip cruise from New York to Bermuda aboard the Holland America liner *Veendam*. The June 13 departure date, immediately following the end of our ten-year-old-old grandson's school year, fit our schedule perfectly.

Living aboard a luxury liner for seven days fit the other requirement of a work-free environment. Everybody could do as they pleased during the day: exercise in the gym, swim, read, eat when and what they wanted for breakfast and lunch, and sightsee individually wherever they wanted to go in Bermuda. But at the end of each day, it was planned that everyone would gather on the veranda of Helen's and my cabin for cocktails, followed by a sumptuous dinner together at one large table in the ship's main dining room. The invitation clearly stated that all expenses would be charged to my credit card. Nobody was to spend a nickel of his or her own money.

Initially my invitation received a lukewarm response. Work schedules interfered for some. Janice's responsibilities as a lawyer for Liberty Mutual had increased with her firm's recent acquisitions. Dana was busy seeking new clients for a start-up business in restructuring bankrupt enterprises. Nick's freelance job with a publishing house peaked in June, as did his girlfriend Emilie's duties at the Metropolitan Museum of Art, swarming with early-summer tourists. Doug and Marc had other travel plans. But in the end, everyone but Marc made it.

On board the *Veendam*, there were two so-called "formal nights" requiring all the men to wear jackets and ties. Dana I had often seen nattily turned out in business garb. But I had rarely seen Nick or Doug wearing anything but work or sport clothes. I couldn't help noticing how handsome the two of them looked dressed to the nines. But what struck me most as I surveyed all eight of us sitting around the table was the fiercely independent spirit of each individual, including our grandson. How did we ever stay glued together

through their sibling rivalries and all the other minor
feuds and squabbles suffered by most families, including ours? How, however, didn't matter. The fact is we
did, and that looms as the most important thing to me
as a ninety-year-old man in a world that seems to be
coming apart. As Havelock Ellis wrote: "Life is beautiful and ideal or the reverse, only when we have taken
into our consideration the social as well as the family
relationship."

It's often the most trivial incidents that are remembered best. Sitting there at the dinner table, I was also
reminded of a few minor events that revealed the spirit
of independence, or was it stubbornness, early on in
the life of each son. During the Woodstock era when
Dana was applying to colleges, he had long hair worn
in what Helen and I regarded as an unflattering pony-
tail. He also shunned neckties for an open shirt bar-
ing a few sprouting chest hairs. He insisted on keeping
that disheveled appearance, despite our pleadings
otherwise, for his meeting with a group of local Yale
grads who were interviewing prospects on behalf of
their alma mater's admissions committee. As might be
expected, he didn't get into Yale. But he was admitted
to Dartmouth, known for its more rough-hewn, outdoor students.

Nick was even more strong-willed. He decided a
week before graduation from Princeton that he didn't

want to turn in his senior thesis on James Joyce, a requirement for getting his degree. "I've gotten a good education," he argued. "What difference does the degree make?" It took me two days down on the campus, hammering on him to turn in the thesis. In retrospect I think he was right, though I didn't see a happier man than Nick at graduation.

We were living in Hong Kong when Doug entered the freshman class at the University of Wisconsin. Unbeknownst to us, ten thousand miles away, he felt lost in that huge student body. Entirely on his own he worked out a mid-year transfer to St. Lawrence, a small liberal arts college in upstate New York, from where he eventually graduated.

Perhaps the most independent-minded of all was our youngest son Marc. When he was only twelve he was arrested, much to his mother's horror, for selling firecrackers to some neighborhood boys. Helen insisted to the juvenile court judge that he didn't mean to break the law. It was simply his budding entrepreneurial spirit that today serves him well. Many parents I now see resist the independence of their children, forgetting how they as youngsters yearned for it.

Sometimes I wondered if my traveling for work deprived the kids of having a father around, especially when they were teenagers. During the Vietnam War there were five- and six-week stretches when I was away from our apartment in Hong Kong. On the other hand, as a result of my job, all four sons got to travel extensively themselves, a penchant for which they still retain.

Being a father and raising a family was farthest from my mind sixty-five years ago when I was preparing to muster out of the army at the end of World War II. I had no idea then how vital, stabilizing, and fun having a wife and family could be. As a twenty-five-year-old major in the Philippines I wanted only one thing: to be a "Young Falcon," as those journalists were called who interwove their personal adventures with their reporting. It was a style of writing started by Richard Harding Davis, the daring young scribe who had covered the Spanish-American War with such verve and color for the Hearst newspapers.

I had first become enthralled with that idea while reading Vincent Sheean's fascinating memoir, *Personal History*. The book was required reading in my freshman English class at Dartmouth. Even then, I identified with Sheean, who at twenty-seven was one of those Young Falcons in China on assignment for the North American Newspaper Alliance. He landed in the Yangtze River city of Wuhan in 1927, the seat of the revolutionary government following the overthrow of the Manchu Dynasty. Soon after his arrival the political ferment there reached a boiling point and then turned violent because of the sudden collapse of the early coalition between Mao Zedong and Chiang Kai-shek. Chiang then established his own Nationalist capital in Nanjing.

Sheean had immersed himself in the fight between the two opposing Chinese leaders after falling under the spell of Mikhail Borodin, Stalin's high adviser sent from Moscow to help create a Red China. When Sheean veered off into a lot of analysis, his editor cabled him, "You are sending too much about politics." As he admitted in the memoir: "I had not been sent to China to write about politics or the revolution, but to engage in some kind of personal enterprise, capers, or high jinks that would carry on the tradition of romantic adventure."

It was the thought of living a life of romantic adventure that seized me as I looked for a job, ideally covering China and the war between Mao and Chiang. For a few nights a recurring dream even took me flying with falcon wings from one publication to another in New York City, seeking such an assignment.

When I finally did land the job in China in 1946 as a transportation officer for the United Nations Relief and Rehabilitation Administration, the position I settled for after being turned down by all the news organizations, I had a serious girlfriend—an attractive and bright American, working as a secretary for UNRRA in Shanghai. For a while, we talked about marriage. But a year and a half later when I was hired by *Life* to be its China correspondent that idea evaporated.

For the next four years I was consumed by my war reporting for *Life* in China, Korea, and Southeast Asia, followed by coverage of the Cold War in Europe. My lifestyle was simple: I owned nothing more than I could cram into one small carry-on bag. When I look around our apartment today, filled with Oriental antiques and other treasures collected by my wife on our travels, I momentarily yearn for those simple, one-suitcase days. But then as my gaze falls on each individual piece, it brings back memories of an exotic place we visited together.

I also had no permanent residence, preferring to stay in hotels and press clubs wherever the job took me. That way I was entirely mobile, able to fly instantly to wherever the action dictated. And the world offered no shortage of action. Several times I barely escaped being killed by surprise attacks, or raids that went askew.

As an example, during the Communist uprising in Malaya (now called Malaysia) in 1948, I was with a special British-led police unit, crawling cat-like through a rubber plantation in a dawn ambush, when they flushed out the rebel leader, Lau Yew. They shot and killed him and several of his followers.

Suddenly, fifty or sixty more rebels materialized on the rim of the saucer-shaped plantation, and soon the whole hollow exploded in a blast of Bren guns and rifles firing in rapid bursts. I dove into a shallow brook trickling through the plantation, smashing my eyeglasses and mashing the pieces of glass into my face. I was afraid to raise my bleeding head, as the ear-splitting exchange of machine-gun fire sizzled above me. Luckily a company of Gurkhas came to our rescue. The rebels fled, leaving bodies strewn between the slanting rows of freshly tapped rubber trees.

It was that kind of action that kept the adrenaline surging through my veins, suppressing any thoughts of seeking a wife. For that matter, no sane woman would have tolerated a husband involved in those escapades.

Besides, I was working so hard there was almost no time left for socializing. Writing didn't come easily for me. I sweated over my copy, turning out uncounted drafts of an article before cabling it to my editors in New York. Although *Life* was a picture magazine, it contained considerable text, some of it appearing under a byline, which I eagerly sought by following Vincent Sheean's example of turning some stories like the Malaysia incident into a personal adventure.

During the free time between assignments, of which there was very little, I also lived a bit recklessly, occasionally picking up the kind of girl in Shanghai,

Seoul, Saigon, or Bangkok that you'd never bring home to mother. I also ate the local food, often bought from noodle vendors on the street, and drank the local tap water. So it wasn't surprising that, while covering the crucial million-man Battle of Huai-Hai that led to Mao's conquest of China in 1949, I came down with that virulent combination of typhoid fever and yellow jaundice, which kept me in the hospital in Shanghai for a month. Luckily I did get better. Otherwise, as the doctors warned, I would have been considered dangerously contagious like the infamous Typhoid Mary, and sent home for special treatment.

Covering Asia was fraught with other health hazards. During the Korean War in the winter of 1950 to '51, frostbite was almost as big a threat as the invading Chinese. The twenty-five-below-zero temperature posed the damned-if-you-do, damned-if-you-don't decision of whether or not to spend the nights zipped up snugly inside your sleeping bag or on top of it. Zipped up in it, and unable to spring into action, you risked being bayoneted in a surprise attack by the enemy. Sleeping on top of it you risked having your toes freeze, turn black, and drop off.

Eventually, when I found myself back in the New York office in 1951 amidst all the smart and attractive young *Life* researchers, the thought of marriage didn't seem so alien. When my former Shanghai boss,

Bill Gray, made a point of introducing me to Helen Rounds, a pretty young picture editor on the magazine, as somebody I should date, it didn't take me long to fall in love. And the feeling seemed to be mutual. Yet I was still reluctant to relinquish my independence. So when it came time to leave on a couple-of-years' assignment as the *Life* bureau chief in Germany—an important career step up for me—I made the mistake of going alone. As the celebrated Swiss psychiatrist Carl Jung claimed: "When love rules, there is no will to power; and when power predominates, there love is lacking. The one is the shadow of the other."

Tension from the Cold War was at a peak, and once again I became consumed covering the action— mainly hair-raising escapes by Eastern European refugees fleeing across the Iron Curtain. I don't believe I had ever explained to Helen before we were on the *Veendam* how riveting these stories were. Or how they could have sidetracked me from marrying her.

First, there was a Czech railroad engineer who became so intent on fleeing the Communists that he drove his steam locomotive through the steel barricades at the West German border, hauling three cars of flabbergasted passengers to freedom with him. When I arrived at the scene each passenger was still faced with the dilemma of whether or not to stay and seek political asylum or ask to be sent home. In the end about a third remained in Germany, while the rest returned to Czechoslovakia, including the panic-stricken conductor, whose decision I couldn't comprehend after he told me he might be shot for failing to stop the train.

Then there was the cockamamie assignment dreamed up by my editors, of trying to liberate Associated Press correspondent Bill Otis from a high-security Communist prison in Prague. Otis had become a Cold War *cause célèbre* after being arrested on trumped-up charges of espionage. A former FBI agent approached *Life* in New York with the implausible proposition that for $10,000 he could bribe Otis's guards and spirit the AP man to a hideout in Austria where I would be waiting to interview him. It didn't occur to my editors that Otis, a correspondent for the AP, might not want to give the exclusive story of his incarceration to *Life* rather than to his own employers. In the end that didn't matter. Instead of springing Otis the FBI man vanished with *Life*'s money, but only after leading me on a three-week-long chase up and down the Czech border. Traveling so steadily, it didn't register that the letters from Helen had stopped coming.

But the stories kept coming. One of the most tragic involved a twelve-year-old Hungarian boy who had been so traumatized by the sight of a Russian soldier shooting his mother and father that he could no longer hear or speak. I discovered him in a refugee camp near Graz in the southeast corner of Austria. For four years he had wandered from house to house. Finally, he fled alone on foot to Austria, where I found him huddled in a corner of the camp, ignored by the other inmates as deaf and dumb. Not even the camp authorities knew much about him. But when I showed him a little attention, the boy perked up. Then with considerable coaxing he drew some pencil sketches of his parents' execution, followed by more drawings of his adventure-filled flight. His crude illustrations provided *Life* with a poignant story that needed few words. When I think back about that boy, I realize how sheltered a life our sons led.

Frank White, the *Time* bureau chief in Germany, had come down to Graz to cover the same story for his magazine. But none of the wire services or newspapers had gotten onto this touching tale, so that night after wrapping up our scoop Frank and I decided to celebrate. We hired a horse carriage, loaded it with beer, and set off on a tour of Graz, tossing the empty bottles into the street behind us. Along the way, we found two giggling girls who were happy to join us. Finally, with both our beer supply and the girls gone, a police car intercepted our carriage, and hauled Frank and me off to jail.

Back in Munich the next day, I had a serious talk with myself. "Your editors may be happy with the work you're doing. But you are thirty-two years old and your personal life is leading nowhere." Worse yet, I was obviously veering off on a path of self-destruction.

Then I asked myself the question that had been nagging at me ever since I arrived in Germany: "How could you have gone off and left Helen?" Especially with all those eager young reporters in the "bullpen," as *Life*'s newsroom was called? Even more worrisome, I had recently heard through the grapevine that she was dating one of them.

That was enough. I picked up a phone in the Bayerischer Hof Hotel and called Helen in New York. Three weeks later, on May 19, 1952, we were standing side by side in the *Standesampt* (marriage bureau) in Frankfurt taking our wedding vows in German. An American consular officer and two *Life* photographers, David Douglas Duncan shooting black-and-white and Jim Whitmore shooting color, were present to record the event. Later that day, most of the *Time* and *Life* correspondents and photographers from London, Paris, Rome, and Bonn, joined us in a huge outdoor celebration.

With that wild group, as you might imagine, we were not going to escape on our honeymoon very easily. My German car was a small two-cylinder, two-seat convertible called a *Gutbrot* (Good Bread), which, like some motorcycles, ran on a mixture of gas and oil. As we jumped in and I stepped on the gas for a quick get-away, the wheels spun with a ferocious roar. But the car didn't budge. Four of the guys had lifted it up onto cinderblocks, leaving the wheels an imperceptible inch off the ground. After that false start we drove the tiny car all the way across the Alps to Italy, stopping by mountain streams to fill the steaming radiator with water.

Although Helen had flown to Germany to marry me without any apparent hesitation, looking back I think she rightly had some reservations—she took a six-month leave of absence from her picture editor's job at *Life* instead of resigning. In any case, there we were fifty-eight years later, cruising to Bermuda, still very much married and surrounded by the wonderful family we had raised—without question, our greatest achievement.

During all of our world travels neither of us had been to Bermuda before. Even so we decided to spend most of the week aboard the *Veendam* reading, relaxing, and enjoying all the amenities of the ship. We left it to the "kids," as we still refer to our middle-aged sons, to do most of the sightseeing.

We also wanted to use some of that quiet time aboard to talk about our future. The problems of growing older, the things we should have expected, had just recently hit us unexpectedly. As Walt Whitman came to realize:

Youth, large, lusty loving—youth full of
grace, force, fascination,
Do you know that Old Age may come after
You with equal grace, force, fascination?

To answer Whitman, we didn't, but we should have. In the past year our lives had changed radically. The macular degeneration in Helen's right eye, coupled with a devastating case of shingles in her left eye, suddenly left her unable to read. Almost worse, she had to stop the faux painting of furniture, an art that she studied and taught at the world-famous Isabel O'Neil Studio of the Painted Finish in New York. Her low vision and some minor neurological problems also affected her balance, making it necessary, when we were out in the street, to walk hand-in-hand. But that wasn't so bad. We viewed ourselves as a pair of young lovers, not hobbling oldsters.

Helen's sudden and severe setbacks had changed my life as well. I became a part-time caregiver and full-time chauffeur, shopper, cook, and reader. But as the humanitarian Albert Schweitzer wrote: "Life becomes harder for us when we live for others, but it also becomes richer and happier." Naturally, I was happy to be in good enough physical shape to help Helen after all she had done for me and our children.

In spite of Helen's ailments, we vowed on the *Veendam* not to succumb to an assisted living establishment, and to tough it out at home. We hated the thought of being surrounded only by old people like ourselves. Happily, as so often happens, the friends of our children had become our friends too. So we were just as accustomed to associating with their generation as our own. Also, our top-floor condo fortunately has a private elevator, and an extra bedroom and bath that could accommodate a full-time helper if that ever becomes necessary.

Our lives, however, are still remarkably full, and on the ship we congratulated ourselves on all of the things we are still able to do. As Aristotle both asked and answered: "What grows old? Gratitude." And indeed we are grateful that we can take the train to New York City, and do frequently, to attend the opera, visit friends and museums, and to attend cultural events at the Century, a club for artists, writers, and musicians. Most important of all, I am still able to drive, even at night if necessary. In fact, I went out and bought a new Ford Escape on my ninetieth birthday. (Our beloved fifteen-year-old Explorer had finally died, although we had counted on it outliving us.)

I asked the dealer, "Do you get many ninety-year-old guys buying new cars?"

"You're first," he replied. That made me feel good, although I suspected he might be buttering me up to clinch the sale.

One of the books I brought along to read on the cruise was the new biography of our former boss called *The Publisher: Henry Luce and His American Century*, by Alan Brinkley. As I read aloud the story of this remarkable man and friend, Helen and I were reminded of what an important role he had played in both of our lives—even our children's, who may not have been born with silver spoons in their mouths, but had Tiffany silver porringers to eat out of, engraved "From Henry R. Luce and the friends of his parents at Time Inc." And when the kids came of prep school or college age, it was his policy to give them a company-paid trip once a year to wherever we, their parents, were stationed abroad. I suspect Luce recalled those painful years of separation when he was a student at Hotchkiss and Yale and his missionary parents were living in China.

The book brought back many memories. I recalled how sometimes when Luce visited a bureau he confided in the bureau chief like he was a son (there were no women bureau chiefs then), sometimes sharing personal concerns and confidences that were embarrassing. On one of his visits to Chicago, where Helen and I were transferred from Germany, Luce and I were riding down Michigan Avenue in a rented limo on the way to see Mayor Daley. Suddenly, he turned to me and said: "What am I going to do about Clare?"

"Oh Lord," I thought, "the man's got marital problems and he wants my advice."

Not so. It turned out that Luce worried that his multi-talented wife had become bored after serving as ambassador to Italy.

Before I could answer he said: "Guess I'll call Foster," meaning the then-Secretary of State, John Foster Dulles, "and see if he can do something for her."

Luce did indeed call Dulles and Clare was soon named ambassador to Brazil. Unfortunately, during her confirmation hearings she announced publicly that Senator Wayne Morse of Oregon, one of the committee members opposing her appointment, had probably been kicked in the head by a mule. The firestorm that caused in the Senate led her to withdraw.

During Luce's same visit to Chicago, Helen thought it would be nice if we invited him for dinner in our apartment for a home-cooked meal. There in a relaxed environment he could meet all of the eighteen bureau reporters, photographers, photo lab technicians, and secretaries, right down to the office boy. We had a long dining room table but it could barely squeeze in eight people on each side, and one person at each end. Luce, of course, was seated at the head of the table, and I as bureau chief at the other end. Helen opted to serve and not sit.

The dinner started off badly. A discussion of Midwestern politics disintegrated mainly because of Luce's pronounced Republican leanings. Besides, one of the photographers drank too much brandy and accidentally bit into his glass snifter, spurting drops of blood onto the white tablecloth. By that time Luce was impatient to end the evening. But suddenly his mood brightened. "What do you people do for fun?" he asked.

Just a few days earlier we had all chipped in a total of two thousand dollars and bought a racehorse named Stepping Stone II. Luce was intrigued, instantly displaying his insatiable curiosity. He peppered us with questions about the horse's breeding, trainer, past record, and future prospects. All we knew was that the critter hailed from Nassau in the West Indies, where he'd won a few small purses. But there he had always run clockwise, as was the custom in the Bahamas.

"Harry, we haven't any idea how he'll do running in the opposite direction on American tracks," I explained. Luce didn't care. He insisted on buying a hundred-dollar share. Eventually, Stepping Stone II won two races at Waterford Park in West Virginia, and Luce got back $46 on his investment.

Some of the meetings with Luce could be very uncomfortable. Especially when it came to the selection of his key editors. In 1959 after transferring from

Chicago to the New York office as a senior editor of *Life*, I would receive an occasional handwritten memo signed HRL suggesting a story or complimenting me on one that I had originated. He rarely contacted me by phone. But one day he called around 1 p.m. and asked if I was free for lunch. "Yes," I exclaimed eagerly, although I was just about to step out the door for lunch with one of my writers.

He took me to the Racquet Club, a majestic structure on Park Avenue, where it seemed the dining room tables were placed about fifty feet apart so conversations couldn't be overheard. Immediately he began probing with questions about what I would do if put in command of *Life*. "Would you fire the deadwood all at once," he asked, "or gradually over time?" "Is there too much text?" "What about the design?"

It was a game Luce was known to play, pitting one editor against another. But it was embarrassing because in this case the entire staff knew that George Hunt, a tall ex-Marine with a commanding presence, was about to be appointed managing editor. If you looked in George's office at any time of the day or night, there he was, writing in longhand on lined yellow pads his version of a new *Life* prospectus—a Luce requirement for any editor about to take over one of his magazines. Besides, Luce probably knew that George and I were close friends and that we and our wives had spent many weekends together on George's forty-foot boat fishing for giant tuna and swordfish. George, I assumed, had even told Luce that he was planning to promote me to assistant managing editor in charge of the magazine's news coverage, once he took over. So the last thing I would want was to derail George's anticipated appointment. Nevertheless, Luce persisted in probing deeper on what changes I would make in *Life* if put in charge.

It was already getting dark when we finished lunch. As we stood up to leave, Luce said, "I'd appreciate it if during the next few weeks if you'd send me your thoughts on a new prospectus for *Life*." I never did. And Luce never asked for it again.

Helen and I talked about what might have happened had I followed up on Luce's request. George would have been furious, very possibly ending my career at Time Inc. for being disloyal. We also conjectured on what prompted Luce to play that game. Brinkley's book mentioned how Luce and Briton Hadden, before founding *Time* together, had engaged in a "bruising battle"—which Luce lost—for the chairmanship of the *Yale Daily News*. Luce was devastated. "My fondest college ambition has been unachieved," he was quoted as writing to his parents. Helen and I decided that his game of pitting one editor against another might have been a carryover from the sour

grapes he suffered following that painful loss to Hadden. In my case the game ended harmlessly. George
became ME and I became assistant ME, a title I was
as proud to have then as I am now of husband, father,
and grandfather.

I must confess that the implication of Luce's probing did excite me. It came at a moment in my career
chase when the job loomed more important than
anything else. In my old age I realize how foolish that
was—how much more in life was yet to come as our
four sons grew up and began careers of their own.
Wrote Tennyson, whose poetry often reflected his concern with growing old:

> *Old age hath yet his honor and his toil.*
> *Death closes all, but something ere the end,*
> *Some work of noble note may yet be done—*
> *Learn to appreciate unexpected small surprises.*

Our nicest surprise was the belated arrival of a
grandson. For several years after our four sons had
reached their forties, we were reconciled to not having any grandchildren. Then, almost as a miracle it
seemed, William arrived—a bright, healthy young boy
whom we are counting on to perpetuate the family.

As Helen and I discussed Brinkley's book, we mar-
veled at the detail about Luce's personal life—even

his sex life—that the author dredged up during the ten years he spent doing the research and writing. But most intriguing to us was comparing our memories of the editor-in-chief with Brinkley's descriptions of him. Our impressions, although limited, were firsthand, while his were drawn mainly from letters, memos, and other archival material.

Once at an intimate dinner at the Luces' New York apartment, with only three or four other editors and their wives present, we were surprised how Luce, himself, took all the drink orders and passed around the hors d'oeuvres, while Clare just sat there, seemingly disinterested in the guests. After reading Luce's biography, it occurred to us that the little dinner party might have taken place on an "off day," in what the author described as Harry and Clare's "on-and-off relationship." The "off" days became most noticeable, according to Brinkley, after Clare discovered the torrid romance Luce was carrying on with Lady Jean Campbell, Lord Beaverbrook's young niece, who had been hired as a researcher for *Life*.

My most vivid memory of Luce—and one that hasn't dimmed in the passing years—occurred on Friday, November 22, 1963. A dozen of us were sitting around the long boardroom table with him when the maitre d' poked his head in the door and interrupted the weekly editorial lunch. "The president is on his way out," he announced sonorously. Then he disappeared.

"What president does he mean?" I wondered. "And on his way out of where?" I had often attended Luce's Friday lunches. Never before had this polite headwaiter barged in and stopped the editor-in-chief in mid-sentence.

A moment later the phone rang. *Time*'s managing editor picked it up. "My God!" he exclaimed. "Kennedy's been shot."

I was sitting directly across the table from Luce. He stared down at his half-empty plate in silence. Though a staunch Republican, he was an admitted admirer of the vigorous young president. The day after Kennedy's nomination, we editors were amazed to learn that he had sat up half the night watching the Democratic convention with Joe Kennedy, Jack's father.

For a minute nobody around the table spoke. Finally, Luce looked up and in his twangy, nasal voice said, "Well, we better get back to work."

For me that meant flying out to *Life*'s central printing plant in Chicago and throwing out big chunks of the magazine that had already gone to press, substituting eyewitness accounts and photographs from Dallas. These included frames from the now-famous eight-millimeter movie film showing the actual assassination, taken by a local dressmaker, Abraham Zapruder.

But I couldn't help remembering how Luce showed no anger, no sorrow, or any emotion at all as he made the practical suggestion that "we better get back to work." And when I think of him today, those few words still ring in my ears.

Helen and I realized we owed much to this man Luce. Our marriage would not have taken place had we not both been a part of his publishing empire. The exotic places we lived, the adventures we had, the close friends we made and still cherish, the world leaders we met, our travels, even our cruise organized by the Time-Life Alumni Society, all stemmed directly or indirectly from Luce. It's not that he dominated our lives, because we saw him too infrequently for that. Neither was he particularly warm and engaging. It was because of Luce, though, that our lives—also the lives of our sons while they were growing up—were so full and exciting.

When Luce died of a massive heart attack in 1967, I was flattered to be one of the editors picked to serve as an usher at his funeral held at the Madison Avenue Presbyterian Church in New York. And as I write these final words of what is my ninth book (and last, as I've promised Helen), a bronze bust of Luce rests on the corner of my desk. Inscribed on its base is: "Roy Rowan, winner of the 2004 Henry R. Luce Award for Lifetime Achievement in Journalism." I'm prouder of that award than of any other honor received during my ninety years.

Acknowledgments

First and foremost I want to thank my wife, Helen, for cheerfully accepting the long hours I spent secluded with my word processor instead of being with her. And also for the times when we were together that my mind was elsewhere thinking about this book. My four sons, Dana, Doug, Nick, and Marc, and my daughter-in-law Janice, though they may not realize it, helped mightily to keep me feeling young as I eased into my nineties.

I am deeply indebted to William P. Gray. He not only rescued me, a frustrated relief worker and aspiring young journalist in China, and recommended me for a job with Time Inc., but introduced me to Helen before he died prematurely at the peak of his career. And I must thank *Time, Life,* and *Fortune* magazines for sending me all over the world for thirty-five years, gathering the stories told in these pages.

Three individuals involved with the publishing of this book deserve my gratitude. Janice Goldklang, executive editorial director of Lyons Press, brought the unfinished manuscript to the attention of her book selection board. Executive editor Mary Norris made a number of excellent suggestions while editing the manuscript, and Ellen Urban, its project editor, proved invaluable in seeing the book through the production process.

I would also like to thank Nancy Perry Graham, a former colleague at *Fortune* and now editor and president of the AARP magazine, for urging me to keep going after reading the first three chapters. My long-time friend Carey Winfrey, editor of *Smithsonian* magazine, also deserves my gratitude for publishing a short essay of mine taken from the first chapter that similarly helped to spur me on.

And last but not least, I appreciate that Carol Mann, my literary agent of some twenty-five years, never gave up on *Never Too Late*.

About the Author

As a foreign correspondent, writer, and editor for *Time*, *Life*, and *Fortune* magazines, Roy Rowan came to know many of the world's most powerful political, business, labor, and military leaders.

He was born in New York City on February 1, 1920. Even as a young boy he aspired to be a reporter. After graduating from Dartmouth College in 1941, where he was a stringer for the *Boston Post* and *Spring-field Republican,* he spent four years in the army, serving in New Guinea and the Philippines, in all ranks from private to major. After the war, unable to land a job as a journalist, he joined the United Nations Relief and Rehabilitation Administration, running truck convoys with food and clothing to the devastated Nationalist and Communist-held villages in Central China. While working there he sold a few articles and photographs to American magazines, including *Life*, which hired him in 1947 to cover the last two years of Mao's revolution. He later covered the Korean and Vietnam wars, as well as the Cold War in Europe and civil rights movement in the United States.

Retiring from Time Inc. in 1985, he has since written numerous freelance articles, including one on the top fifty Mafia bosses in the United States that earned him a death threat, and another about homeless people based on the two weeks he spent living on the streets of New York. This is his ninth book: The others include *The Intuitive Manager,* an international best-seller, and *Chasing the Dragon,* a memoir about his China days that has been optioned by Universal Pictures, as well as *Throwing Bullets, Solomon Starbucks Striper, Surfcaster's Quest, First Dogs, Powerful People,* and *The Four Days of Mayaguez.*

Roy and his wife, Helen, live in Greenwich, Connecticut, and Block Island, Rhode Island. They have four sons and one grandson.